CHAOS AND ORDER IN INDUSTRY

CHAOS AND ORDER IN INDUSTRY

BY

G. D. H. COLE

AUTHOR OF
"SELF-GOVERNMENT IN INDUSTRY" "SOCIAL THEORY"
"LABOUR IN THE COMMONWEALTH" ETC.

NEW YORK
FREDERICK A. STOKES COMPANY
PUBLISHERS

PREFACE

MOST of this book appears for the first time; but in certain parts of it have been incorporated, in a more or less altered form, articles which have appeared in the following periodicals: *New Statesman*, *Daily Herald*, *Venturer*, *Guildsman*, *The New Republic*, *The Dial*, and *The Journal of the American Institute of Architects*.

G. D. H. COLE

CHELSEA, *March* 1920

CONTENTS

APPENDICES

CHAOS AND ORDER IN INDUSTRY

CHAPTER I

THE CAUSE OF STRIKES

A MAN healthy is a man : a man sick is an organism. We become conscious of the workings of our physical system in proportion as that system is disturbed or out of order. However little society may resemble an organism in many ways, it is like it in this. Society, that is, the ordinary man in society, becomes actively conscious of the industrial and economic system only when he finds by experience that something has gone wrong, and that the system is not functioning properly in relation to the life of the community as a whole.

We are acutely conscious of industry to-day because industry is in a mess, because its normal working is constantly interrupted by disputes between the various parties now concerned in it, and because, as consumers and users of its products and services, we directly experience the results of its disorder. No one can afford at the present time to say that he is not interested in the industrial system, if only because the industrial system, without being greatly interested in him, is constantly deflecting the

I

ordinary course of his life, and, by concentrating upon itself the attention of the best brains in the community, preventing the doing of other things that need to be done, and causing even the best-laid plans which ignore its peculiarities to break down.   We must attend to industry, because, until we have got industry reasonably organised, it is not of much use to attend to other things of equal importance and certainly of greater ultimate interest.

It is not because industry is in itself interesting, attractive or engrossing to the ordinary man that the ordinary man must sit up and take notice of it.   It is even because it is, to him at least, uninteresting and unattractive.   He does not want to think about strikes and profits, or methods of industrial organisation.   There are other things much nearer to his heart, and in his opinion, which matters most, much better worth thinking about.   But he is coming to realise that, unless he sees that the industrial chaos is converted into an order which the workers in industry will accept, the future will hold for him, not merely discomforts and disturbances, but acute privations and perhaps the dissolution of the society on which the realisation of his personal desires depends.

Thus far the majority of intelligent persons have got already.   They have realised that industry and the industrial system are matters of personal concern to them in their everyday life.   But many intelligent persons have got no farther.   Having realised that industry matters, they have merely based a strong opinion about industry on their existing prejudices and presuppositions, and have made no real attempt to think out for themselves what is wrong with industry, or what ought to be done to set the industrial house in order.   A class prejudice, an assumption inculcated in the home, the school, the church, or the newspaper, an elementary instinct of pugnacity seem good enough grounds on which to base an attitude towards the warring factions in the industrial world.

Slowly, however, this attitude is changing. There is a steadily increasing curiosity about the position, the motives and the capacity of the various parties to the industrial conflict, and an increasing willingness to examine and consider the solutions put forward by various schools of thought, and the actual programmes and policies of industrial and political bodies. Slowly, the lump of prejudices is being leavened by reason, and an attempt is being made to understand why industry is in its present chaos, and how the ordinary citizen can help in the task of reconstructing it.

At present, this growth of the spirit of reason is obscured by the fact that it is accompanied by an even more rapid strengthening of the opinions based on prejudice. For the majority of the people, a violently prejudiced opinion is the half-way house from apathy to reason. They begin by taking no interest : then circumstances force them to take an interest and, having no background of knowledge, they fall back on prejudice as a substitute. Then gradually some at least of them gather knowledge, and prejudice is slowly pushed back into the hinterland of their minds.

Such bodies as the Middle Classes Union in this country and the " White Guards " of continental countries are the organisations of prejudice. The average peer or " clubman " who blacklegged during the railway strike did so, not because he understood anything of the industrial situation which had led to the strike, but because the instinct of class prejudice was strongly awakened in him.

No doubt, it will be said that the Middle Classes Union and the blackleg peer have their exact analogues in the world of Labour. I am not concerned to deny it. The organisation of prejudice is not a class monopoly. My point here is that those who adopt a course of action on prejudice can be led subsequently to reason about the action which they have taken, and that this gradual conversion of prejudice into reason is one of the most powerful instruments of social progress.

I am instituting a comparison, not of individuals, but of stages of organisation when I say that, in working-class organisation, the movement is now steadily from prejudice to reason, whereas the middle and upper classes are only now advancing from apathy to prejudice. This means that the " better " classes are at present becoming more consciously reactionary, because they are attempting to translate their prejudices into a positive policy. It does not mean that the working-classes are becoming more moderate ; for reasonableness and moderation are by no means the same thing. Indeed, the prejudices and presuppositions of the workers in many cases made them " moderate " ; for prejudices base themselves on the past, whereas reason points to the future.

The conflicts between Mr. Robert Smillie and the Duke of Northumberland may serve to point the present contrast. Mr. Smillie may reason well or ill ; but he certainly reasons and presents a closely reasoned case. Even those who would cast him for the part of the ἄδικος λόγος would hardly deny that he is a λόγος of some sort. But the Duke of Northumberland gained the tumultuous applause of Belgravia and the *Morning Post* not by reasoning, but by an impassioned outpouring of all the prejudices of the old order. Short-sighted reformers may grieve at the awakening of the reactionary prejudices of the hitherto apathetic upper and middle classes : those of longer sight will not grieve, because they will realise that anything is easier to fight than apathy, and that it is easier to reason with a White Guard (if only with a machine gun) than with a clubman taking his afternoon nap over the *Morning Post*.

Of course, all the roads from prejudice to reason do not lead in the same direction. Reason is a big and a divided country, and there are provinces in it of wrong reasoning as well as of right. The *Morning Post* reader or White Guard who marches from prejudice to reason will not necessarily arrive in the province of just reasoning ; he may well find himself with the Geddeses and the Federation of British Industries in the province of unjust reasoning. But, whereas in the country of prejudice falsehood has the advantage of truth, the tables are turned in the country of reason, and the unjust reasoners, however powerful, are but an Ulster minority, whose resistance may be long and stubborn, but cannot in the end succeed.

Why do strikes take place, and why, in all industrialised countries, are they rapidly increasing in frequency and in dimension ? The answer of upper and middle class prejudice is that strikes are caused by persons called " agitators," or nowadays " Bolsheviks," who possess a magical power of persuading the workers to respond to their destructive designs. This is equivalent to saying that there is no material cause at all ; for, when it becomes necessary to explain why there are these " agitators " and " Bolsheviks," prejudice falls back either on the explanation of original sin, or else upon the infinite regress in some such form as this :

Bolshies here have Russian Bolshies striving to incite 'em,
Russian Bolshies German Bolshies—so *ad infinitum*,

which does not carry us far towards a solution.

No person, however, in whom the light of political reason has even dawned, will long remain content with the "Bolshevik" or "agitator" explanation. He may continue to hold that matters are made worse by "agitators"; but he will soon realise that agitators would agitate in vain unless there were something substantial about which to agitate. Whatever part, therefore, he may assign to "Bolshevism" in heightening and deepening unrest, he will be compelled to look elsewhere, in the economic system itself, for the fundamental causes of unrest, the causes which make it possible for agitators to agitate successfully.

As soon as we begin to examine the economic system from a human point of view, and try to see how it must appear to the ordinary worker engaged in industry, the difficulty is to understand not why unrest and strikes exist, but why they are not far more prevalent. For not even those who hold that the present order of things is inevitable dare, as a rule, to put up a reasoned case in favour of it as just or pleasant for the ordinary man. Prejudice may be content with crying that the rights of property are in danger, and rally the property-owners by this elemental cry; but the unjust reasoners of capitalism have a much harder job to make a plausible case. They are driven more and more to defend the whole capitalist system on the principle of the philosopher who said that "This is the best of all possible worlds, and everything in it is a necessary evil." Private enterprise may result in an unjust distribution of wealth, and in a huge waste in the processes of production; but it is "necessary" in order to afford an "incentive" to produce. Autocracy in industry may be in conflict wth the democratic principles which we profess in politics; but it is necessary in order to secure efficiency. The wage-system may be unjust and it may be impossible really to value human services in terms of wages ; but it is necessary in order to stimulate the workers to produce. There is hardly a reasoned defence of the capitalist system which is not based upon the conception that " everything in the world of industry is a necessary evil."

To the workers, the evil in these cases is naturally more obvious than the necessity, especially as a good many of the minor " necessary evils " of capitalism have already yielded to their assaults and proved, so far from being necessary in any absolute sense, to be not even necessary to the continuance of capitalism. Moreover, they have seen the capitalists themselves rapidly abandoning what used to be regarded as the central and essential "necessary evil " of the whole system — competition, or the crushing-out of the weak by the strong. Can we be surprised if, with these examples before them, they are sceptical of the necessity of evils which apply not to the whole human race, or to all classes in society, but to the special class of wageworkers under capitalism ?

It would be astonishing that the capitalist system survives at all, were it not for the fact that prejudice is still stronger than reason, even among the organised workers. Prejudice is always telling the workers that they always have lived under capitalism, and it is therefore only natural that capitalism should continue. It is only reason that slowly makes headway and suggests the possibility of a different industrial and social order, while indicating also that a new social order cannot be built in a day, or by the mere destruction of an old one.

The reason of the workers therefore leads them at the least towards a highly critical examination of the " necessary evils " of capitalism, and at the most towards a repudiation of their necessity, and the putting forward of a constructive alternative. For a time, criticism may have been stifled by lavish promises, made by Ministers and by employers, of a new heaven and a new earth ; but the revelation when the war ended of the unchanged attitude of Capitalism and of the Government's complete lack of a constructive policy soon reawakened the critical faculties of Labour, and the steady leftward drift of the workers began.

It will be agreed that there are few signs in the world at present of the coming of that brotherhood of the " classes " which some prophets foretold as the result of the war for democracy. From almost every country comes news of Labour unrest on a large scale, and from most countries of serious strikes often developing into civil disturbances. It is, of course, easy to exaggerate the signficance of such movements, whose precise importance the continued activity of the various censorships and the breakdown of the ordinary forms of international communication have made it very difficult to ascertain. But enough reliable information comes through to make it certain that revolution is at least a possibility in at least half the countries of Europe in which it has not already occurred—to say nothing of the chances of further, and more real, revolutions in such countries as Germany.

The plain fact is that all over Europe, and to an increasing extent in America also, the armies are mobilising for something like a class war. Economic movements have a rapidly growing tendency to become also political, not only because the workers possess a greatly increased power and are far more conscious of it, but also because their economic claims are animated by a steadily deepening hostility to the whole capitalist order of society. Not only do the workers feel stronger, they have also a growing feeling that capitalism is insecure. The greatest barrier to labout unrest before

the war was the widespread conviction that capitalism
was inevitable—that it had been in possession ever since
the workers could remember, and that there were no signs
that it was likely to come to an end. To-day most of the
world, and the workers perhaps most of all, have lost the
feeling of certainty about anything. We have come
through such changes already that no change for better or
worse now seems altogether impossible. Empires, apparently strong and impregnable, have perished almost in
a night ; new nations have arisen ; one great country is
actually governed by extreme Socialists, and several others
largely by Socialists of a milder type. After the fall of the
Habsburgs, the Hohenzollerns and the Romanoffs, after the
coming of Soviet Russia and, for a time, of Soviet Hungary,
who, whatever his attitude towards these things, will dare
to affirm that revolutionary social changes are impossible
in his own country ? Who will hold an untarnished faith
in the permanence and inviolability of the old order ?

In this country, we have so far been less affected than
any continental people by the prevailing unrest. But
here, too, the same forces are at work. Long after the
termination of hostilities, how different is our economic
situation from that which was foreshadowed by the
optimists who told us of the blessings of "reconstruction."
We, too, are a prey to insecurity ; we, too, are grown
more tolerant of daring adventures and more credulous of
Utopian speculations. Our manufacturers and traders,
however grandiose the plans which they lay for the future,
lack confidence. They know not what the morrow may
bring forth, either at home or abroad. Accordingly, they
tend to put off till to-morrow what they would do to-day
if they felt secure, with the result that unemployment
remains a problem and, in the absence of rightly directed

production, prices continue to rise.   The workman is equally
uncertain of the future, and therefore, as well as because he
feels stronger in his organisation, more ready to take the
risks and more disposed to listen to the advocacy of a new
social order.   It is, however, true that in this country we
are only at the beginning of a process which has gone much
farther on the continent of Europe.   There, the dissolution
of the old order is manifestly in progress ; here, the dissolution is only vaguely present so far in men's minds and
has not yet seriously affected their everyday actions.

The fundamental causes of the world-wide unrest are
mainly economic.   Some peculiarly bad clause in the
Peace Treaty, some blunder of the politicians, some manifestation of militarist reaction, may prove to be the spark
which will set the world ablaze.   But the fundamental
cause of the conflagration will lie deep down in the economic
system.   The workers of France or Italy or Great Britain
will rise in revolt not so much because injustice is being
done to the workers of Germany or Hungary or Russia,
as because in every country it is becoming increasingly
difficult, as the Coal Commission has abundantly shown,
for the workers to live any longer under an economic system
devoted primarily to the making of profit.   This is not to
say that a majority, or anything like a majority, is consciously demanding the overthrow of the capitalist system.
Socialism of any constructive sort remains, probably in
every country, the creed of a minority.   But even the majority which has not attempted to formulate a constructive
opinion has changed.   The pre-war industrial system rested
upon the general acquiescence of the workers in the subordination of their personality to the needs of industry as
interpreted by capitalists and employers.   It was possible
only because it was able to treat Labour as a thing instead of

a number of persons, and because Labour, though it kicked occasionally, as a rule acquiesced in that treatment. To-day, nearly every one has a higher conceit of himself than he had before. Nearly every one makes not only higher material claims, which are hard enough for capitalism to satisfy, but also higher human claims, which it has no means at all of satisfying, and which most of its protagonists do not even attempt to understand. We are face to face with the fact that the war has taught the workers in almost every country to assert their human claims by putting forth the vast economic strength which hitherto they have not known how to use.

To-day, men are refusing any longer to believe that they were made for industry, and are asserting vehemently that industry was made for all men, and must adjust itself to, and comply with, human needs. That is the real meaning of the world-wide unrest, the real moral of the repeated strikes, from whatever immediate causes they may spring.

The question, then, for the peoples in all countries is whether the economic and social system can transform itself so as to comply with the new human standards of value by which it is being judged. If it cannot, it will go to pieces, not perhaps this year, but next year or the year after, or at least within the next decade. Many people see that this is true of a large part of Europe, and yet believe that this country is somehow mysteriously immune from the coming epidemic of social and industrial revolution. There could be no greater mistake. What is true of Europe is true of us ; and it is certain that we must either undertake the complete overhauling of our industrial system or else plunge slowly after our neighbours into a chaos out of which a better order may arise, but which will certainly first cause untold suffering in every class.

> It may be we shall rise the last as Frenchmen rose the first,
> Our wrath come after Russia's wrath, and our wrath be the worst.

If we are to escape such an ending to our knight-errantry on behalf of " world democracy," we shall do well to set our house in order. But where and how are we to make a beginning ? The system of private profit has us, like our neighbour nations, in its toils. Our Ministers of State are still declaring that they desire to see high profits, because high profits are essential to the rapid and successful development of industry. Our employers have still no suggestion for a remedy for social ills beyond a reiteration of the demand for increased production. Yet surely it is obvious to anyone who looks with half an eye at the industrial situation that the problem of production is only part of a general psychological problem, and that there can be no solution of it, and no creation of industrial efficiency, unless the idea of production is related to the idea of service. If we want efficiency, we must persuade the workers that it is worth while, and their bounden duty, to do their best ; but this we cannot do while we still ask them to work under a system which, from any moral standpoint, is utterly indefensible. The only appeal which can restore the world to good order is a moral appeal ; and such an appeal, under present conditions, we simply have not the right to make. It is true that our position is in this respect certainly no worse than that of other nations; but it is a scant consolation if we must all perish together for our sins.

There is no need to take a sensational view in order to emphasise the gravity of the strikes which are now epidemic in every industrial country. One strike epidemic after another may pass without achieving any big result. But that does not make them any the less serious ; for they are manifestations of a general sense of insecurity and dissatisfaction which is everywhere and every day growing stronger and more insistent. It is out of economic movements that, under present conditions, political movements are almost bound to proceed ; and, even if our present troubles blow over, we can be sure that others will follow unless the root evils which create them are removed. Yet where in Europe to-day, if we except the Soviet countries, is the Government with either the courage or the power to tackle one of these root evils ? Can we be surprised if we drift ever faster towards the rapids ?

CHAPTER II

MOTIVES IN INDUSTRY

ONE "reconstructs" all sorts of things—a broken-down motor-car, a halting sentence or a defaulting company. At present, our politicians are engaged in the congenial—and very much larger—task of "reconstructing" a world in ruins. It is a difficult, and it should be an inspiring, task ; but, as in the case of most really big jobs, there are more ways than one of doing it. Without pushing the comparison too far, we may fairly follow a little farther one of the comparisons made above—that of " reconstructing " a company.

In view of their business training, that is almost certainly the way in which our statesmen look at the problem of "reconstructing" the world—for, after all, they would tell us in their more candid moments, the world is only an unusually big group of businesses with the Allied Powers as a sort of trust competing with the rest—Allied Powers Ltd. beating Central Powers Ltd. out of the market.

There are two ways of reconstructing a business. One way, quite frequently practised on both sides of the Atlantic, is directed principally to restoring the market price of the shares and lining the pockets of the chief share-holders. For the purposes of such a reconstruction, it is usually quite unnecessary to interfere with the existing methods of carrying on the business, however inefficient they may be. What is necessary is only to get the right people on to your side, to make the public believe that all is well—in short, to " restore confidence " in the stability of the business without in fact making it any more stable than it was before.

It is that "confidence trick" that our politicians are trying to play off on us to-day under the name of " Reconstruction."

The other sort of reconstruction is far more difficult and far less often attempted. It involves finding out what is really wrong with the business, questioning its very basis and, if necessary, altering fundamentally the principles upon which it is conducted. It is occasionally undertaken even in business ; but it is very unpopular with the shareholders, because it usually includes the writing down of the shares from their nominal to their real value.

That is the sort of reconstruction we need in industry to-day. We have to write down the share of the rich in the proceeds of industry to the amount which represents the real value of their services, and we have to enforce drastic changes in the methods by which industry is managed and controlled.

The time has come both to question everybody's income by the test of public service, and to establish a new industrial order by substituting democracy and self-government for the existing conflict of " master and servant."

Naturally, this is not the sort of reconstruction our rulers have in mind. To say nothing of their interests, their very imaginations are the slaves of the old order. They cannot think of the State except as a large business, and they cannot think of business except in terms of dividends and Stock Exchange prices.

Their idea of the reconstruction of Britain is to put back

industry into the hands of those who mismanaged it before the war, and to rebuild, as soon as may be, the whole structure of private profiteering and capitalist control.

Such schemes of reconstruction ignore a vital change in the situation. The conducting of industry for private profit and the vast inequalities of wealth which went with it were possible only because Labour acquiesced in a system over which it had no control. The worker was treated under that system as a mere raw material of industry ; and he allowed himself to be so treated because he had not fully realised the possibility of any alternative. He was not even a sleeping partner in the firm of Britain and Co. ; he was not recognised as a partner at all.

The situation has changed radically during the war. Whatever may have been the case five years ago, it is certain that now the only way of "restoring confidence" is to place the management in new hands, and at the same time to "squeeze out the water" from industrial capitalism.

Labour to-day is rapidly coming to realise its power, and to refuse any longer to acquiesce in its dependent status in industry. It is demanding the right to a share in the control of industry, and to the appointment of those who are to exercise industrial authority. It proposes a real reconstruction which will place the management of industry in the hands of the workers themselves.

This is, indeed, the only way out of the difficulty. If Capitalism can no longer "boss" Labour, it is impossible for Capitalism to carry on. There remains the alternative that the State should buy out the capitalists, issuing them Government stock in exchange for their shares, and should then carry on on their behalf. But, if the workers will no longer work for private capitalists, will they work any more readily for a capitalist State ?

The real question in industry to-day is a question of *motive*. On what motives are we to rely in future for securing that the necessary commodities are produced and the necessary services rendered ? That is the fundamental problem which lies at the basis of all real reconstruction, and it is a problem which most schools of social thought and action seem afraid even to seek or suggest a solution.

Before we attempt to answer this test question, it is necessary to state bluntly and categorically the nature of the motives on which we have hitherto relied to secure the application of effort to the task of production. According to all accepted ethical principles, these motives have been predominantly evil, although they have been supplemented, in a certain degree, by motives which are good. Thus, in the case of the capitalist entrepreneur, it has been generally assumed, and openly stated by the economists, that the dominant motive, the "incentive to produce," is personal gain. It may be contended that this is not in itself a bad motive, and I willingly agree that there is nothing bad in the desire to secure a " competence " for oneself and one's dependents. But it is not on the desire to secure a " competence " that we have relied, but on the desire to acquire riches, in other words, on the motive of personal greed.

I do not, of course, mean that all capitalists, or even the majority of capitalists, are in fact actuated solely or even mainly by this motive. There are many other motives, good and bad, which actually operate on the capitalist in industry to-day. But I do say that our social system is so ordered, or disordered, as to throw the main stress and reliance upon the motive of personal greed, and that, however amoral economic science in itself may be, those who use economic science to justify the present system are

2

in fact relying upon the motive of personal greed to secure the application of enterprise to production.

This attitude was, of course, far more nakedly avowed in the early days after the industrial revolution than it is to-day. Readers of contemporary social and economic literature and speeches, or of Mrs. Gaskell's novels, or of Mr. and Mrs. Hammond's graphic presentation of the mind of the period in *The Town Labourer*, will not need to be convinced on this point. But even those who admit the brutality of the capitalist mind in the early nineteenth century, may not be so ready to agree that the position remains essentially the same to-day. Nevertheless, it does. The motives on which the industrial system relies to-day, although they are more disguised, are essentially the same as those on which it relied a century ago. There has been, no doubt, an advancemnt in the status and economic position of the workers ; some protection has been afforded by industrial legislation, and a great deal more by Trade Union action. But has a single important step in this advance been made except in the teeth of the opposition and prognostications of ruin of the great majority of capitalists, and has the whole process up to the present time altered in any way the basis or the motives upon which modern industrialism rests ?

Let us put the case concretely. If a fish dealer thinks that he can make a higher profit by throwing part of a catch into the sea and selling what remains at a higher price than by selling the whole catch at a low (but still a remunerative) price, will he hesitate in the majority of cases ? Year in and year out fish dealers actually make this choice, and choose the higher profit irrespective of the public advantage. If a manufacturer can make a higher profit by producing luxuries than by producing necessaries, will he not in almost all cases produce luxuries with an un-troubled conscience ? If a capitalist ring expects a higher profit from restricting than from expanding output, will it not usually restrict output and pat itself on the back for its commercial acumen in doing so ?

I do not say that the idea of the public interest is wholly absent from the minds of those who follow these vicious courses, or even that it has no influence at all upon their conduct. If the anticipation of profit from two possible courses of action is approximately equal, the average business man will probably choose that which in his opinion is most conducive to the public interest. But that he will, in the vast majority of cases, make profit the first considera-tion, is a fact which simply does not admit of doubt. Indeed, he will assume as a matter of course that he should do so, and will very likely be grieved and outraged by the suggestion that his action is anti-social and immoral. He will probably say, especially if his business is a joint-stock company, that men do not go into business " for their health," and that he " has to consider the shareholders first."

And it is quite true that, in many cases, he has, under the present system, no alternative. I am attacking, not individuals, but a system which no individual, unless he is very rich or does not care about money, can easily disregard. The average business man is probably no worse morally than the average man in other spheres of society, except in so far as his occupation is actively demoralising ; he is a part of a system, and that system is immoral and beastly.

In so far as our industrial system is a result of conscious choice, we must plead guilty to having chosen to rely, for the drive and direction required in industry, principally upon the motive of greed.   But this motive has necessarily operated with the requisite intensity only upon a few. In the case of the many " rank and file " workers employed in industry, the principal reliance has been placed upon a quite different motive.   The mass of workers have quite literally been driven to the factories by sheer economic necessity, and the motives upon which we have relied to make them submissive workers have been motives of fear—fear of hunger, fear of unemployment, fear of sub-mersion in the hopeless *strata* of society.

These motives operated more or less " satisfactorily " as long as the workers were isolated and unorganised and felt the immense inferiority of their forces to those of the economic system whose slaves they were.   Indeed, they still operate " satisfactorily " where, and in so far as, these conditions are still realised.   But the huge extension of Trade Union organisation, and the greatly increased self-confidence which the workers have derived from the sense of a solidarity based stably on Trade Unionism, have funda-mentally altered the position.   It is a plain fact that the workers in the great industries are no longer afraid enough to ensure the continuance of production under the old system.   They are more and more feeling that they possess the power to challenge capitalism in the economic field, and their Trade Unions afford them an economic resource, inadequate but still substantial, upon which to depend during the struggle.

This is a position which we have reached to-day.   The control of Capitalism over Labour is breaking down, and the economic system is staggering under the blows admin-istered to it.   In other words, the old motives in industry are no longer effectively operating.

This imposes upon us absolutely, whether we will or no,

a definite decision concerning the motives upon which we propose to base the economic system of the future. A choice of system is always primarily and fundamentally a choice, not of the machinery to be created, but of the motives to which the principal appeal is to be made. It is true that if certain economic machinery is created, an appeal to a certain set of motives will follow logically upon it ; but such an order of procedure is not choice, but blind submission to material forces. In the realm of will, which should be the determining factor in social organisation, choice of motives precedes, and points the way to, choice of machinery.

Before, then, I even begin to discuss the various schemes of industrial organisation which are dealt with in succeeding chapters, I want to get quite clear about the basis on which we wish industrial organisation to rest. To make choice of a certain set of motives will not, of course, mean that machinery corresponding to these motives can be brought suddenly and completely into existence. We have to build on the basis of things as they are, and to do our best to change them gradually into things as we believe they ought to be.

What, then, is to be the dominant set of motives—the motives which we must endeavour to make dominant—in the new industrial order. For greed and fear, I believe we must substitute the motive of free service. Instead of appealing to men's material desires and terrors, we must appeal to their ideals. We must induce them to work, to put their backs into the task of production, by letting them see clearly that their work is for the community, and by asking them to give freely of their best in the common service.

To my mind, the first condition of such an appeal is the

elimination of private profit. While the position remains as we described it earlier in this chapter, that is, while it continues to be regarded as a perfectly normal and proper proceeding that the forms and amounts of production should be determined in accordance with the maximum expectation of profit, and not at all in accordance with the greatest human need, it is a sheer impossibility to make an appeal to the rank and file worker to put his best at the disposal of the community by working well and, for instance, increasing his output. He will reply, with perfect propriety, that the main result of his working harder at present will be, not to benefit the community, but to put more money into his employer's pocket, and sometimes even to harm the community by doing so, as by intensifying the diversion of production from necessaries to luxuries, or by increasing capital accumulations at the cost of under-consumption. The elimination of private profit, or at all events the de-position of the "profiteer," [1] is not the only condition of installing public service as the dominant industrial motive ; but it is an essential condition. There may be various ways of doing this ; but as the principal means, so far as the vital industries and serivces are concerned, national and municipal ownership hold the field. Other methods. may be appropriate in certain other cases ; but the nationalisation of the great industries is a first condition of a successful appeal to the workers to put their hearts into the service of production.

The second condition is no less important. Service is only real service when it is free service, and the service of

---

[1] I use the word in its original sense, to include all who order production for profit, and not in its journalistic sense, which confines it to those who make an "excessive" profit, whatever that may mean,

the public under the new conditions must be as near to " perfect freedom " as the imperfection of all human institutions will allow. If we abandon coercion by the fear of hunger and unemployment as the motive to industry for the many, it is of no use to dream of replacing it by other forms of coercion. We must abandon the idea of external coercion to labour, and rely upon the willingness of men to work as soon as they can see that their work is worth while. Coercion is breaking down because, although a mob may be coerced into positive action, a self-confident and organised group of any size cannot be so coerced. A group can, of course, be repressed if there is a stronger organised power against it. The organised workers may even be forced into the factories ; but no power on earth can make them work, or at least work well.

In the past, a real choice may have lain between successful coercion in industry and an appeal to free service. Now, there is no such choice. Coercion cannot succeed in providing the consumer with the goods and services which he needs, and a further attempt to apply it merely means a deeper descent into the abyss of industrial unrest, ca' canny, and perhaps, before long, civil war. An appeal to free service may still be regarded as a " leap in the dark " : I prefer to regard it as a " tremendously big," but splendid, " adventure." I do not suggest that the whole change can be made in a moment : indeed, the main purpose of this book is to suggest some of the stages by which it can be made in various industries with the minimum of dislocation. But I do suggest that our only alternative to this adventure is a gradual but speedy descent into the abyss.

Moreover, we must adventure boldly and at once. Time is against us, and the old order is dissolving into anarchy and chaos much faster than we are at present building the new. When I suggest that the change will be gradual, I am far from meaning that it can be slow. It must be rapid and decisive, if the work of construction is to be put in hand quickly enough to forestall the impending collapse.

For I do sincerely believe that the present economic order is breaking down, and that its definite collapse is a matter not of decades, but of years. And I am concerned to avoid, if it is possible to avoid, the sharp break of social revolution in the extreme sense. I do not want to see our present society collapse suddenly as from an earthquake, and its members to be left among the ruins to build up afresh, amid such difficulties as the Russians are facing to-day, a better social order. Not that I despair of the ultimate results even of such a catastrophe. The new social order could, I believe, and would in the end be built. But how many men and women would die and suffer meanwhile ; how many children would be killed or stunted ; how many priceless possessions of civilisation would be lost. " Through terror to triumph " is a desperate remedy, and if there is a chance, as I am sure there is, of re-building society without an intervening period of chaos, we should be fools and criminals to miss that chance. But unless we begin at once, and take the chance before it is gone, to that desperate remedy we shall come.

Men, admirably disposed and full of public spirit themselves, will tell you with every appearance of conviction that any appeal to the public spirit of the many is bound to fail in the sphere of industry. Industry, they say, is unpleasant, and men will only work because they must. Surely the whole history of society gives the lie to the theory that men will only do unpleasant things if they are compelled to do them. Again and again men have gone to works as unpleasant as those of war without compulsion. For example, how many thousands of men and women are there in the Labour movement—not to mention any other movement—to-day, who are doing hard, dull, unpleasant work at high pressure for no form of monetary reward ? If men do not give such ungrudging devotion to industry, is not that because in industry the right appeal —the appeal to free service—has never been made ? I believe that men will work for an ideal as they can no longer be made to work for fear. And, if I am wrong, then who is in the right, and what hope is there for society at all ? For, if men cannot be forced to work and will not work for an ideal, it is plain that they will not work at all. If that is so, the sooner some straying planet crashes into the earth, the better will it be for the human race.

CHAPTER III

THE RECONSTRUCTION OF PROFITEERING

I

THE POLICY OF THE GOVERNMENT

DURING the war, the British State became by far the largest employer of labour in the British Isles. It did this, not only by establishing State control over railways, coal mines, munition factories and other essential industries, but also by building, equipping and manning for itself national factories, national shipyards and a large fleet of standard ships. In addition, it necessarily accumulated in its own hands vast numbers of lorries, trawlers and other coasting vessels, locomotives and other items of transport, vast quantities of stores, and a vast reserve of raw materials which it had bought in foreign markets.

No sooner was the armistice signed than hasty preparations were made not only for the speedy abandonment of control, wherever possible, over privately owned industries, but also for the immediate disposal of the national industrial property which had been acquired during the war. No sooner was the General Election over and publicity once more comparatively safe, than the policy was made known in a series of the most startling announcements. The national factories were to be either sold or dismantled : the national shipyards were advertised for sale : a Disposal Board was set up to get rid of other forms of national property ; and, not content with at once abandoning the control of shipping, the Government sold out the standard ships, both those which were in commission and those which were still being constructed, to what the *Times* facetiously called " the shipping community." Moreover, Sir Eric Geddes, who was the Government spokesman on this question, publicly announced to a meeting of the Associated Chambers of Commerce that the Government's policy was not to use any national factory for the purpose of producing articles in competition with the private manufacturer. At subsequent meetings between the Trade Unions and the Government representatives it was made plain that this applied even to articles required by the Government itself for its own consumption, where such articles could be produced by private firms. For instance, the Government refused to use a particular national factory for making telephones on the ground that private firms could supply the numbers required. This was done in face of a vast unsatisfied public demand for telephones, which the Post Office was blandly informing the public that it was not in a position to supply.

Even before this policy had become generally known, the workers in certain particular national factories were made aware of it by receiving wholesale notice of dismissal, and were thus threatened with being flung upon the unemployed market. These workers, with the backing of the Labour Party and their Trade Unions, thereupon approached the Government and asked it to retain the factories in question, and use them for the manufacture of articles which were urgently required, such as locomotives and railway wagons, of which there is a world shortage ; door-frames, window-frames, stoves and grates, and other articles vitally necessary for the rehousing of the people ; dock-gates and other articles of hydraulic and electrical engineering, and a host of other necessary products. They urged the Government to retain the splendidly equipped national aircraft factories, and so prevent the creation of a huge new monopoly in the manufacture of aircraft. Every request was useless : the Government persisted in dismantling some, and selling privately or by public advertisement others, of the national factories. In this way it contributed handsomely to swell the numbers of the unemployed, whom it had then expensively to relieve by the payment of out-of-work donation.

Moreover, this policy of industrial suicide was applied not only to the new factories and shipyards which the State had acquired during the war, but also to those which it had possessed long before. Woolwich Arsenal had its staff drastically and progressively reduced, in spite of the action of the Trade Unions, which urged that its magnificent equipment should, in the national interest, be fully utilised in producing goods such as locomotives and telephones which were admitted to be urgently required.[1] A little later, the same method was applied to the Royal Dockyards, which ought clearly, from the time when further naval construction became unnecessary, to have been fully employed in building national ships to make up for some of the huge losses caused by the submarine campaign. In both cases the cry against competition with

[1] Twelve months after the armistice, an order for locomotives was placed with Woolwich Arsenal by the Government, as the result of strong pressure from the Woolwich Shop Stewards' Committee and the Labour Party in Parliament.

private enterprise was raised, and thousands of workers were thrust forth workless from the national establishments in order that not even the slightest inconvenience might be caused to private capitalists in search of excessive profits.

Even more startling was the policy adopted by the Government in relation to shipping. Control over private shipping practically ceased to exist at the end of March 1919. This was in itself remarkable enough, seeing that the world economic situation, then as much as during the war, made an international system of rationing of foods and raw materials indispensable for some time to come. But, in addition to relaxing control and abandoning it altogether in the majority of cases, the Government insisted on divesting itself of the ships which it had caused to be built for the national use and at the national expense, and handed over these ships to the private shipowners at a time when the shortage of shipping offered an unparalleled opportunity for extortionate freight rates. The result was that, instead of falling, average freight rates rose steeply ; for a fall in the rates previously charged for uncontrolled tonnage space was far more than offset by a steep rise in the rates for tonnage which was previously under control. As the shipping interests in this country, as elsewhere, are closely combined, the Government obviously played straight into the hands of a vast and dangerous monopolistic interest.

Indeed, this was everywhere the distinguishing feature of the Government's policy in relation to reconstruction. The war afforded an enormous opportunity for the growth of capitalistic combination, and there is no doubt at all that during the years of war the extent of combination among firms in this country at least doubled. This meant a huge increase, not only in the economic, but also in the political power of capitalism, and it is not too much to say that the new Parliament elected in 1918, and the Government itself, were completely dominated by the big vested interests. "Big Business" won all along the line, and the guiding hand of governmental reconstruction became the hand of massed capital.

The slogan of the official policy was "No interference with private enterprise," which means "No interference with private profiteering." Because "Big Business" was at the helm of State there must be no public competition with the private producer, even in the supplying of Government orders, and the State must strip itself naked of all its industrial capital and use the proceeds of its sale in order to "fake" a budget which would for the moment relieve the pressure of taxation on the rich.

At the same time, the public began to hear now of pledges given to "Big Business" during the war—pledges not revealed at the time, and only becoming known when they fell due for fulfilment. During the General Election of 1918, Mr. Winston Churchill announced that the Government intended to nationalise the railways. Not long after the election was over, Lord Claud Hamilton announced the previous existence of a pledge that the present system of railway control should continue for at least two years after the final end of the war, and the decision of the Government to adhere to that pledge. It was generally believed that the premature abandonment of control over shipping and other industries and the evacuation of the national factories and shipyards were also due to pledges given in secret on the first institution of control. Experiments of vast social value, such as the Wool Control Board, were ruthlessly sacrificed in the interest of private profiteering. The urgent need for the development of a co-ordinated ystem of railway, road and canal transport was not met, because pledges had been given to the railway companies ; and there are sinister rumours of other pledges no less disastrous, but still to be revealed.

Faced with the universal opposition of Labour to this policy of national surrender to " Big Business," the Government attempted certain evasions. For instance, it attempted to give a large and liberal appearance to the alienation of the national factories by throwing out the suggestion that some of them should be taken over by the Trade Unions. It seemed at one time possible, even in face of the huge difficulties involved, that a few experiments in democratic control of particular factories would be made by the co-operative movement and by one or two progressive municipalities, if suitable factories could have been secured ; but the suggestion as a whole was preposterous, as Sir Eric Geddes must well have known when he made it. For, in the first place, some of the best factories had already been sold privately to capitalist firms, presumably under pledges given when they were first constructed. Secondly, what funds the Trade Unions have are subscribed for the provision of benefits, and cannot be used for investment in productive undertakings. Thirdly, a Trade Union, even if it could establish the most efficient system of workshop management, would stand no chance under the conditions imposed by the capitalist system of success in the competitive market. It would not only be systematically undersold, even at a loss : it would be held up, or blackmailed, for the raw materials, machinery, etc., which it would have to procure from other private firms. Even progressive employers in the engineering trades have sometimes found the difficulty of maintaining a low cost of production in face of the hostility

of the big combines ; and certainly these combines would
spare no effort to crush out of existence a Trade Union
competitor.   Sir Eric Geddes represented his offer of the
national factories to the Trade Unions as a concession to
the workers' demand for control of industry ; but he must
have known perfectly well that this demand is not for the
establishment of a few self-governing, profit-making workshops in the midst of a capitalist society, but for the gradual
extension of Trade Union control in industry as a whole,
with a view to a complete change of system.

The Labour Movement did what it could to combat the
reactionary policy of the Government.   One of the Labour
Party's amendments to the Address on the opening of
Parliament in February 1919 expressed " regret that there
is no mention of any proposals for the ships, factories
stores and other properties created or acquired by the
State during the war being retained by the State and used
to their full extent in civil industry in the interests of the
community, and that there is no mention of any proposals
for the acquisition by the State of the railways and canals
and mines of the United Kingdom."   The engineering
Trade Unions protested strongly against the abandonment
of the national factories ;   the railway Trade Unions
headed by the National Union of Railwaymen, pressed
for the nationalisation of railways and canals ;   and the
Miners' Federation asserted its absolute determination
that the mines should in no case be allowed to revert to
private control, and its demand that complete nation
ownership should be at once secured.   These demands are
more fully discussed in other chapters of this book.

The Government's post-war industrial programme presented no single satisfactory feature.   In so far as it
grappled with any of the urgent economic problems con-

fronting the nation, it did so from a purely capitalist point of view, and with a complete disregard for the lessons of war-time experience. Its entire failure to confront the issues of the day in the economic sphere was largely responsible for the outbreaks of industrial unrest, and is responsible to-day for the imminence of far more widespread disputes. It held up the progress of any kind of domestic reconstruction, and ensured that, when " reconstruction " did begin, it should proceed along the wrong lines. And, above all, in playing into the hands of " Big Business," it was not really stabilising the economic system on a capitalist basis, but making certain a struggle of huge dimensions in the near future.

The case of the national factories, ships and shipyards is important, not only because of the hundreds of million pounds worth of public property involved, or of the disastrous effects of their sale or destruction both on unemployment and on international rationing and the international economic situation as a whole, but even more because it illustrates, so clearly that every one can see the point, the general drift of the Government's policy. For the sale of the national ships in particular there was no conceivable excuse except that private capitalism must at all costs be preserved intact. Every other argument pointed with the utmost possible clearness to the need for their retention, and for the development, by means of the national shipyards, of a real national fleet which would both ensure the provisioning and re-equipping of Europe, and prevent the growth of an extortionate monopoly among the private shipowning " community." But in the Government's reckoning, the gospel of " profits first " was triumphant ; to-morrow may come the aftermath in the greatest industrial upheaval in our history.

3

II

Trusts and the Public

Adam Smith once said that " masters are always and everywhere in a sort of tacit, but constant and uniform, combination." Since his day combination among employers has become far stronger and more universal, and has extended its activities to include a far wider range of objects ; but it still preserves at least one feature of its earlier self—it is still largely tacit, or at least its workings are still largely hidden from the outer world. Thus, the Ministry of Labour begins its Directory of Employers' Associations with a statement of the difficulty of securing reliable information about their objects, and the Committee cn Trusts set up by the Ministry of Reconstruction obviously had great difficulty in getting at the facts, and felt even greater difficulty in putting before the world the facts which it did secure.   Indeed, there is a curious irony in the fact that, whereas the Committee's Report insisted most strongly on the need for full publicity concerning the working of trusts and combines, it constantly referred to " a certain association," and carefully refrained from giving names when particular deeds of darkness had to be recorded.   Most curious of all is the fact that the fullest and most circumstantial story given in the Report was quoted from an American official document, and related to the operations of the " Beef Trust," which is mainly an American organisation.   It would be interesting to know why the Committee was so loth to practise itself that publicity which it recommended as the most effective method of dealing with the trust problem.

Certainly it was not because of any doubt in the minds of

the members as to the wide prevalence and rapid extension of industrial combinations. The Report fully recognised the fact that British industries are now largely controlled by associations and combines which, in one way or another, effectively eliminate or greatly reduce competition. It also laid the correct stress on the effect of war conditions in fostering and developing combination, and pointed out in effect that the war departments encouraged combination in order to make easier the organisation of the various trades for national production in war-time. The members of the Committee were also fully alive to the fact that these war-time developments would not, in most cases, be only temporary. Advisory committees established by a Ministry have become trade associations on ceasing to function as advisory committees : methods adopted to apportion output in time of war have been applied to the collective limitation of output in time of peace.

It is to this fact of limitation or restriction of output, as one of the principal methods of trust activity, that the Committee, while it referred to it again and again, did not assign anything like its due importance. Messrs. Hobson, Watkins and Webb, in their separate addendum to the Report, do indeed place this fact in the forefront ; but even they did not reveal its full implications The Report quotes the case of an association, " covering 99 per cent of the total British output of an important steel product," which is based on the assigning to each firm of a quota of the total output. If a firm produces more than its quota, it pays £1 per ton in excess to the pool. If it produces less, it draws 10s. per ton from the pool. In the words of the Report, " one firm that had joined the Association had entirely ceased to manufacture from that time, but had ever since continued to draw a handsome income from the pool." Surely a more remarkable way of creating a new capitalist *rentier* class was never conceived. The firm in question draws its handsome income not merely for no service to the community, but as a reward for refraining from serving the community by useful production. Certainly no Trade Union or group of workmen was ever accused of conceiving so manifestly anti-social a form of restriction of output.

Yet the capitalist is prepared to produce a justification even for such forms of restriction. It is cheaper, he argues, to pension off an inefficient firm than to crush it out by competition. It is simpler, for the Association, to eliminate competition by buying it off than to destroy competitors by undercutting. It is not so clear where the public good enters into this calculation of cheapness.

Yet another nightmare is conjured up by the paragraph of the Report which opens with this encouraging sentence : " There was a general agreement among representatives of Associations before us that one of the beneficial results of the formation of Associations sufficiently powerful to control and maintain prices in the Home market was that it enabled British manufacturers to extend their output by selling their products at a lower price, or even at a loss, in foreign markets." The chairman of " a number of important Associations " " had no doubt at all that it would be a sound policy to sell in foreign markets at a loss." In other words, it is necessary to have combinations in order to compel the British consumer to pay such high prices as will enable British capitalists to sell their goods dirt-cheap to foregin consumers. If this is the theory of trade held up before us, clearly it follows that the British consumer must retaliate by encouraging the dumping of foreign products in this country to the greatest possible extent;

If the conclusion is absurd, does it not follow logically from the premisses ?

This Government Report, taken together with its valuable appendices, for which the Committee timidly disclaimed responsibility, proves clearly that price-fixing combinations of capitalists are now almost general throughout the major productive industries. The Government Report on Bank Amalgamations showed no less clearly that trust combinations are equally general in the sphere of finance. They are extending rapidly even to those spheres of industry and commerce which have hitherto been immune. In fact, it is safe to say that, so far as the major part of industry and commerce is concerned, the fixing of prices by home competition is already a thing of the past. But this is not because the community has decided that competition does not work fairly, or because it has devised a new method of securing justice between producer and consumer ; it is simply and solely because the capitalist interests have discovered, as sooner or later they were bound to discover, that combination pays better than competition. Though the leaders of the big combinations claim that their combinations will not harm the consumer, it is clear that they regard the service of the consumer and of the community, as capitalism has always regarded it, as a mere by-product of profit-making.

What, then, are the suggestions put forward for coping with this vast menace of syndicated capitalism ? The Ministry of Reconstruction's Committee on Trusts was not particularly helpful. It merely suggested the establishment, under the Board of Trade, of machinery for the investigation of particular complaints of the activity of trusts, to be followed, where necessary, by State action, presumably through Parliament. As Messrs. Hobson,

Watkins and Webb pointed out, this proposal obviously falls far short of what is necessary to safeguard the public interest. Is the Board of Trade, which has always taken up the standpoint of the capitalist producer, likely to prove an effective check upon forms of combination which it has clearly shown that it approves ? Is Parliament, with the Board of Trade as its instrument, likely to prove more effective ?

If these methods are certain to fail, how is the problem to be dealt with ? The plain fact, as America and other countries have already discovered, is that if capitalism is allowed to remain in existence it is really impossible to dictate to it how it shall organise itself and what methods it shall pursue. Legislation did not make the conditions which created the regime of free competition ; it only followed some distance behind, aiding and abetting the economic forces which it could not control. Similarly to-day the forces making for combination are too strong to be combated, and no power of Parliament will prevent combination from spreading through every industry in the country, save perhaps the smallest and most primitive. The only question is, Who is to wield the monopoly power which comes of combination ? As long as private ownership remains in industry, so long, with or without State control, the consumer will be exploited, and the capitalist " producer " will continue to pocket an unnecessary surplus, which will be none the less robbery if a proportion of it is handed back to the workers whom he employs. There is no way out save by the rapid extension of public ownership and democratic development of industry.

This was in some measure recognised by Messrs. Hobson, Watkins and Webb in their addendum. They accordingly devoted their attention not so much to the methods of persuading capitalist combines to behave themselves, as to suggesting a constructive alternative to capitalist combination. Where an industry has reached the stage at which effective " trustification " has become possible, there is at least a good *prima facie* case for supposing that it has reached the stage at which public ownership can be applied. The Coal Industry Commission had before it definite suggestions for a model structure and model methods of administration which could be applied to publicly owned industries so as to avoid bureaucracy and provide for the fullest co-operation of the workers and the technical and professional staffs in control. Some applications of this proposal to various industries are discussed in subsequent chapters. With the necessary changes such a model structure and form of organisation ought to be capable of being applied to any industry which has reached the stage of trustified administration. The workmen, at any rate, have been told again and again that the only hope for the restoration of British industry lies in the immediate abandonment of all forms of restriction on output. What is sauce for the goose is certainly sauce for the gander ; if it is wrong for workmen to restrict output, it can be no less wrong for employers to do so. Yet it is perfectly obvious that almost the first act of nine out of every ten effective trade combinations is to take steps for the collective restriction of output, and that no amount of State regulation can prevent trade combinations from pursuing this course. The only escape from restriction of output by both employers and workers lies in substituting a new motive in industry for the motive of profit-making, and in securing the maximum output from industry in the collective interest. That involves public ownership and democratic control of industry, and in these lies the only way of escape from the restriction and exploitations of the great trusts and combines which have so consolidated their position during the war as to be impervious to any less ambitious challenge.

NOTE.—This Chapter was printed before the publication of the sensational series of Reports, dealing with prices and profits in various industries, issued under the Profiteering Act. These Reports give, with a striking amount of detail, corroborative evidence for the conclusions reached in this Chapter. It should, however, be noted that, while the Profiteering Act has been useful in bringing some of the facts to light, it provides absolutely no means of stopping profiteering or of dealing with the profiteers. Despite the disclosures made in the Reports, profiteering continues unchecked, and the attitude of the Board of Trade still seems to indicate that it has no desire to deal with it effectively.

CHAPTER IV

THE GUILD SOLUTION

I

THE GUILD IDEA

MOST people are aware that long ago, in the Middle Ages, industry was organised under a system which is now called the Gild (or Guild) system. They know that for several centuries this was the prevailing method of industrial organisation, and that it gradually decayed before the coming of modern industry, overwhelmed by the expansion of the market, by the substitution of new for old forms of production, by the growing importance of finance, and by the growth of national, as opposed to local, economic and social consciousness. The old Guild system was essentially a local system, and for most people that it is a sufficient reason for dismissing it as irrelevant to present-day industrial problems.

The old localised market, the " town-economy " of which the industrial historians tell us, is indeed gone for ever, though it may be hoped that we shall some day recover the finer qualities which belong to craftsmanship and small-scale production. But, even if we accept, for our time at least, the existence of national and international economy, with their concomitants the world market and large-scale production, there may still be much which we can learn from the guilds of the Middle Ages. For in the great days of the guilds, the ordinary man did achieve a position which he has never occupied in modern industry—a self-government and a control of his own working life which are of the essence of human freedom.

Modern industry is built up on a denial—a denial to the mass of the workers of the attributes of humanity. In the factory of to-day, the workman counts not as a man, but as an employee ; not as a human being, but as the material embodiment of so much labour power. He sells his labour in a " labour market," and in that market an employer or the management of a company buys just that quantity of labour power which can be used for the realisation of a profit. The employer or the firm buys labour power just as it buys electrical power or machinery, and just as an ordinary purchaser buys a pound of tea or a cake of soap. In short, under modern industrial conditions labour is treated as a " commodity," and is bought for the purpose of realising a profit.

Vast consequences flow from this way of treating the worker. Because, in the factory, the worker is present not as a human being, but merely as so much embodied labour power, the worker is not regarded as having any right to share in the control of the factory in which he works. He is there to behave not as a man, but as labour power, to be moved about and used and to have his motions directed at will by those who have purchased his labour. According to the theory of modern industry, not only does the factory belong to the employer to do with it what he will : the workman also belongs to the employer during the hours for which his labour has been bought.

Of course, things do not work out quite like this in

practice. In the bad days of the industrial revolution in the eighteenth and early nineteenth centuries, when the workers were for the most part half-starved, helpless and unorganised, the theory and the practice did almost completely coincide, as they still coincide in the case of the sweated workers in this country or of the downtrodden employees in the mills of India or Japan. But even in these cases the harmony of theory and practice has been on occasion rudely broken ; the workers have rebelled against the conditions of their wage-slavery, and there have been strikes and riots, usually without conscious purpose or final success. In the civilised countries, the workers have gradually organised in Trade Unions, and as they have grown stronger the gulf between theory and practice has widened. The recalcitrance of labour has become more marked and more frequent, and employers have been compelled to bargain collectively with their workers, and to admit their possession not merely of certain human rights, but even of a certain title to a small share in industrial control—usually in the form of certain restrictions imposed by the Trade Unions on the way in which the factories are run. This has meant a growing difficulty in administering industry under the existing system, until unrest has risen to such proportions as to threaten the stability of the system itself. We are now not far off the position when the workers will refuse any longer to be treated as labour power, and when their refusal will compel a complete reconsideration of the principles and the practice of the industrial system.

The growing divergence of theory and practice can have only one end. It is impossible, in view of the present strength and consciousness of Labour, that our industrial practice should ever again be harmonised with the old theory. It remains, therefore, that we should remodel our theory, and make our practice consistent with that new theory.

What is this new theory to be ? It is here that the mediæval guilds can teach us useful lessons. For the only way out of our present impasse is to get back to a position in which every workman can feel that he has a real share in controlling the conditions of his life and work. We must reconstruct our industry on a democratic basis, and that basis can be only the control of industry by the whole body of persons who are engaged in it, whether they work by hand or by brain. In short, the solution lies in industrial democracy.

This democracy must be in many ways very different from the democracy which existed in the mediæval guilds, until the rise of inequalities in wealth made them plunge into oligarchy and finally chaos and dissolution. The mediæval guilds were local, confined to a particular town and its environs : our modern Guilds must be national and even, in many respects, international and world-wide. While preserving in them local freedom and local initiative, we must co-ordinate them on the same scale as the market must be co-ordinated. The epoch of world-commerce calls for national and international Guilds.

There will be a second difference hardly less important. The mediæval guilds were made up of master-craftsmen, with their journeymen and apprentices who could hope one day to be masters, working in independence in separate workshops under conditions laid down by the guild. The modern Guild will be made up, in our time at least, of huge factories in which democratic control will have to be established and safeguarded by far more formal methods than were necessary in the small workshop of the Middle

Ages. Moreover, our modern industries are so interconnected and so bound up one with another, and economic and political considerations are so intertwined, that modern Guilds will have to be far more closely related to the community as a whole than were the mediæval guilds which, it is true, were often most intimately related to the mediæval municipality.

But, with all these points of difference, the resemblance will be far more essential. Modern, like mediæval guilds, will be dominated by the idea of social service—an idea which has almost vanished from the organisation of industry in modern times. They will bring back the direct control of the producer over his work, and will give him the sense, which hardly any one can have in industry nowadays, of working for the community. That, Guildsmen believe, is the secret of getting good work well and truly done.

If we set this ideal of National Guilds before us, how can we set about its realisation. It is made necessary and possible by the emergence and power of Trade Unionism, and Trade Unionism is the principal instrument by means of which it must be brought about. The growing strength of Trade Unionism is beginning to make impossible the continuance of industry under the old conditions : there is no remedy but in making Trade Unionism itself the nucleus of a new industrial order. Our problem, then, is that of turning Trade Unions into National Guilds.

Trade Unions to-day consist principally, though not exclusively, of manual workers. But clearly a National Guild must include all workers, whether they work with their hands or with their heads, who are essential to the efficient conduct of industry. Trade Unionism must therefore be widened so as to include the salariat. This is already coming about. On the railways, in the shipyards and engineering shops and in other industries the salariat is already organising, and is showing an increasing tendency to link up with the manual workers. As the power of Trade Unionism grows still greater, this tendency will become more and more manifest. One part of the building of National Guilds is the absorption of the salariat into the Trade Union movement. Another part, on which I have no space here to dwell, is the reorganisation of Trade Unionism on industrial lines.

As these processes go on, the Trade Unions will continue their steady encroachment in the sphere of industrial control. The divergence between the theory and practice of capitalist industry will become wider and wider, and it may be that we shall find ourselves at last with a practice fitting the new theory achieved without any abrupt or violent transition at all.

What form will this gradual encroachment take? First, I think, the form which it is now manifestly taking in some of the principal industries. The workers will create strong organisations of their own in the workshops and factories (shop stewards' committees, works committees and so on), and will then demand for these organisations positive functions and powers in the control of industry. At the same time, especially in services which are State owned and administered, the Trade Unions will demand a share in control nationally as well as locally. In every direction, the workers through their organisations will gradually demand and secure as much control as they are at present able to exercise. And not merely will the appetite for control grow as it feeds : the competence and the power to control will grow with it, till by a series of stages the functions of industrial management are gradually transferred to the workers' organisations, which will by that time have come to include the whole effective personnel of industry.

This is one side, and the most important side, of the development. But at the same time, the democratisation of industry will be accompanied by a similar gradual democratisation of Society as a whole. The State will be driven more and more to assume the ownership and control of industry, and every step which it takes in this direction will make more important the existence of real and effective democratic control over politics. The National Guildsman believes that industry ought to be controlled by the workers engaged in it; but he believes also that industry ought to be communally owned, and that popular control must be established over the political, as well as over the economic machinery of Society. I have not here the space to deal with this side of the problem fully: I can only say that guildsmen believe that it is impossible to have a really democratic political system while the economic system remains undemocratic, and continues to be based on the denial of the humanity of labour. And, on the other hand, the democratisation of the industrial system will make possible a parallel democratisation of the political machine. The key to political and individual, as well as to industrial, freedom lies in the control of industry, and it is for this reason that the industrial problem occupies its paramount position among social questions. The Guild system, I believe, furnishes the best possible solution of the social problem, because it carries with it the best reconciliation for our time of the principles of freedom and order—principles apparently in conflict, which must be reconciled in any system which is to satisfy our moral striving after personal freedom and co-operation one with another.

II

THE NATIONAL GUILDS MOVEMENT

The objects of the National Guilds movement, as defined in the constitution of the National Guilds League, are " the abolition of the wage system, and the establishment by the workers of self-government in industry through a democratic system of National Guilds working in conjunction with a democratic State." The leading ideas of the movement are therefore those of democratic organisation and self-government in the industrial sphere. National Guildsmen look forward to the time when the various industries and services will be administered each by its Guild, or association organised for common service and including the whole necessary personnel of the industry concerned.

This movement is only a few years old ; but it has made considerable headway not only among the manual workers, but to almost an equal extent among many classes of professional and technical workers. By Marxian Industrial Unionists and others of the extreme left wing of Labour, it has sometimes been denounced as a bourgeois movement of counter-revolutionary tendency. This criticism comes principally from those who refuse to recognise the importance of technical and professional elements in the industrial system, or hold that the existing technicians and professionals are " adherents of capitalism," and that it is necessary to make a clean sweep of them in preparation for a new order ushered in by a purely manual workers' dictatorship.

Guildsmen have hitherto differed widely in their outlook on the social and economic question as a whole. Faith in National Guilds as a form of economic organisation is compatible with many degrees of evolutionary or revolutionary opinion. There are all sorts among Guildsmen from the extreme right which looks to a gradual development of Guilds, perhaps in some cases with the consent of some of the more open-minded employers, to the left which corresponds closely in method and outlook to the Marxian Industrial Unionists. Recently, the differences have shown a tendency to come to a head, and the continuance of both extremes in the League is doubtful.

It will be easier to explain the present orientation of the National Guilds movement if we begin with a short account of its origin and development. It has only gradually attained to its present scope and character, and a number of different and even diverse influences have contributed to its formation. Its earliest manifestation is attributable to Mr. Arthur J. Penty, whose book on *The Restoration of the Gild System* was published in England in 1906. About the same time, Mr. A. R. Orage, then as now editor of the *New Age*, contributed to the *Fortnightly Review* an article on the same subject. Mr. Orage was, and has remained, in close touch with Mr. Penty ; but in his hands the Guild doctrine soon began to follow a new line of development. In 1908, Mr. S. G. Hobson became associated with Mr. Orage on the *New Age*. Shortly after this, the series of articles, most of which were subsequently reprinted in the book *National Guilds : an Enquiry into the Wage-System and the Way Out*, began to appear. This series of articles, which were written by Mr. Hobson with the collaboration of Mr. Orage, gave the National Guilds movement a definite shape, and made it for the first time a practical and constructive force.

4

The essential feature introduced by Messrs. Hobson and Orage—the feature which gave the National Guilds movement its characteristic turn — was the definite association of the idea of industrial self-government with the existing structure of the British Trade Union move‑ ment, and the definite attempt to formulate a proposal for the conversion of Trade Unions into Guilds, that is, of protective organisations of wage or salary earners into managing and controlling organisations, including the whole necessary personnel of industry. I do not mean that the full implications of this association of ideas were at this stage completely thought out, and still less that the practical steps necessary for the accomplishment of the change were clearly proposed : I mean only that the vital idea of National Guilds appeared for the first time, and that the way was thus made clear for further development.

Indeed, at this stage the appeal of the National Guilds idea was almost purely intellectual. No propaganda was proceeding outside the columns of the *New Age*, and the circulation of that journal was almost wholly confined to a section of the "intelligentsia." The great bulk of the Socialist and Trade Union movements remained unaffected ; only in the University Socialist Societies and among middle-class Socialists and professionals did the idea make any progress. It had its partisans among the younger members of the Fabian Society ; but the great bulk of that Society, and practically all the official leaders of the Labour and Socialist movement, were at this time definitely hostile.

In the industrial Labour movement as a whole, the period of which I am speaking was one of great and growing unrest. From 1910 onwards to the outbreak of the war unrest grew steadily and many great strikes took place, including the great railway and transport strikes of 1911 and the mining strike of 1912. This spirit of unrest led to a ferment of ideas in the Labour world. Before 1910 the Socialist Labour Party and the Industrial Workers of Great Britain (offshoots of the American S.L.P. and the De Leonite I.W.W.) had been active in Scotland and some districts of the North of England ; but the atmosphere was unfavourable, and they made little progress. From 1911 onwards the conditions were far more favourable ; but the leadership of the left wing passed for the time rather to movements under the influence of French Syndicalist ideas. The Industrial Syndicalist Education League, led by Mr. Tom Mann, had a considerable transient success, and closely related to it were the various Amalgamation Committees and other " rebel " bodies which are the ancestors of the "rank and file " movements of to-day. In South Wales, the Marxians, through the Industrial Democracy League and the Miners' Unofficial Reform Committee, gained ground considerably, while the foundation of the Central Labour College and the Plebs League gave them a means of propaganda on a national scale. Only at a later period, from 1916 onwards, did the big growth of the (Marxian) Socialist Labour Party begin.

I was a regular reader of the *New Age* from 1906 onwards, and followed with keen interest the successive developments of the Guild idea. I was not, however, at this stage definitely a Guildsman, both because I then disliked the name and because the movement seemed to have too little touch with industrial realities. In 1912 and 1913 I was working on my first industrial book, *The World of Labour*, studying the development of the Labour movement in various countries, and more especially of

Syndicalism in France and of its relation to British Trade Unionism. When my book was published in 1913, I still did not call myself a Guildsman, though I was fully conscious of my close affinity to the *New Age*. At the beginning of 1914 I definitely began to call myself a Guildsman, and with Mr. W. Mellor, the first General Secretary of the National Guilds League, begun to develop Guild ideas by regular articles in the *Daily Herald*. Our object in these articles was at the same time to popularise Guild propaganda and to bring it into the closest possible relation to the everyday work of the Trade Union movement. Towards the end of 1914, despite the outbreak of war, we felt that the time was ripe for a further development, and a small private conference was held in December at Storrington in Sussex, at which a long statement was drawn up formulating our unanimous conclusions on the theory of National Guilds and the steps necessary for their attainment. This conference was followed a month or two later by a second conference at Oxford, where it was definitely decided to proceed to the formation of a propagandist organisation for spreading the Guild idea. A third and considerably larger conference was held in London at Easter 1915, and at this conference the National Guilds League was definitely founded.

Since that time the spread of the Guild idea has been rapid, both in the Trade Union world and among Socialists, and also among the professional classes. The National Guilds League has directed its principal propaganda towards the Trade Union world ; but everywhere its groups include not only Trade Unionists but also professional men, teachers, journalists and even a few employers. It has never been, and has never sought to be, a large organisation. It has concentrated its propaganda work entirely upon the question of industrial and professional self-government, and its aim has been to enrol persons willing to work for the Guild idea with a full understanding of its principle. Its effectiveness has therefore been out of all proportion to its numerical strength : the influence of the National Guilds League has spread far and wide, while its actual membership still remains at a few hundreds. It has the advantage of possessing among its members a considerable proportion of fairly well known writers, and in consequence it is enabled to spread its propaganda over a wide field.

A few instances will serve to explain the extent and character of this influence. The Secretary of the Miners' Federation of Great Britain, Mr. Frank H. Hodges, is a Guildsman. Before succeeding to his present position he moved at the 1918 Miners' Conference a resolution calling for the redrafting of the Mines Nationalisation Bill on Guild lines. This was carried, and the miners proceeded to redraft their Bill accordingly. Early in 1919 they were called upon to lay their proposals before the Coal Commission. Their principal witness was Mr. W. Straker, another Guildsman, Secretary of the Northumberland Miners' Association, who presented before the Commission a scheme for Guild control. Mr. R. H. Tawney, yet another Guildsman, was a member of the Coal Commission, together with Mr. Hodges. Thus, while there are comparatively few actual miner members of the National Guilds League, the policy of the League has to a great extent secured the support of the Miners' Federation.

The same is the case with the railwaymen. The programmes both of the National Union of Railwaymen and of the Railway Clerks' Association are closely in conformity with the proposals of the National Guilds League, both alike aiming at the immediate national ownership of the industry and at the establishment of a system of joint control by the Trade Unions and the State. The programmes of the Post Office Trade Unions are even more closely allied to National Guilds, and in this case also there is a close personal association between the two movements.

A somewhat different instance is that of the National Union of Teachers, which in 1919 carried at its Annual Conference a National Guild amendment, moved by Mr. W. W. Hill, an active Guildsman, by an overwhelming majority. In yet another sphere, the Annual Conference of the Independent Labour Party in the same year redefined its objects so as to bring them into conformity with Guild ideas.

Of course, it must not be imagined that the majority of British workers, manual or professional, are National Guildsmen, or have even heard of National Guilds. The success of Guild propaganda comes largely from the fact that it is working " with the grain," and that circumstances are forcing the industries of Great Britain in the direction of Guild organisation. The conscious Guildsman is still a rarity ; but with or without Guildsmen, the Guild idea continues to make headway in both theory and practice.

III

GUILD PRINCIPLES

The Guild Socialist movement has already created a considerable literature, and books exist upon many different aspects of Guild propaganda and Guild ideas. It is difficult, if not impossible, to give in a few pages any coherent idea even of its general principles and policy; for Guildsmen have always been exceedingly anxious to avoid an extreme dogmatism in the formulation of their programmes. They do not pretend to believe that a Guild Society, exactly as they imagine it, will ever exist, or that they can prophesy the future of social organisation except in the most general terms. When, therefore, they deal in details and sketch out a possible organisation of Guild Society, it is always a possible, and not the only possible, structure which they have in mind. They are prepared to be as sure and definite about general principles as men have a right to be about anything; they are prepared to make definite proposals and suggestions for immediate adoption; but when they go beyond that, they do so tentatively and with the full consciousness of probable error.

With this warning, let me attempt a very brief summary of Guild principles and attitude as I myself envisage them. The central Guild doctrine, as it appears to me, is that the various industries and services ought to be democratically administered by those who work in them. It is, in fact, an attempt to apply to the industrial sphere the principles of democracy and self-government which, in theory at least, are accepted as applying in the sphere of political government.

Guildsmen begin with an analysis of the existing industrial system from the standpoint of the wage-worker. Their initial dogma is that the labour of a human being is not a commodity or article of commerce, and that the present wage-system, in treating labour as a commodity, is guilty of a violation of human justice and of human needs. Guildsmen point out (in common with Marx and many other writers) that the *theory* of the wage-system is that the worker sells his labour power in return for a wage, and in so doing surrenders all claim not only to the product of his labour, but also to the control of the manner in which his labour is used. It is true that this theory is not fully realised in fact, because the collective intervention of Trade Unions in industrial affairs does give the workers, in varying degrees, a considerable control over the manner in which their labour is used. This control, however, is purely negative : it amounts at most to a veto upon the employers' proposals for the use of labour, and not to any positive control by the workers over the conditions of their industry. It therefore necessarily tends to be restrictive rather than directive in its operation.

This system, and indeed the whole existing industrial order, rests upon the willingness of the workers, or the compulsion upon the workers, to go on working for a wage. As soon as the workers refuse to work for wages, and are strong enough to implement their refusal, the wage-system necessarily collapses. The vulnerable point of the capitalist system is therefore to be found in its dependence upon the acquiescence of Labour. The " way-out " of the wage-system, in the view of the National Guilds writers, lies, then, in a refusal by the workers to work for wages. This implies a growth in power and consciousness on the part of Labour, and a transference of the " control of labour " from the employers to the Trade Unions. Guildsmen therefore work for a monopoly of labour and the creation of a blackleg-proof Trade Union organisation, both by a widening of Trade Union membership among the manual workers, and by a progressive inclusion in the Trade Unions of the workers concerned in management, technicians, professionals and supervisors.

The problem, however, is not merely one of widening Trade Union membership : it also involves a reorganisation of Trade Union structure and policy. Guildsmen desire that Trade Unions should direct their policy expressly to the securing of control over industry through the control of Labour. They envisage the strategy of Trade Unionism as a constant encroachment upon the sphere of control at present occupied by the employer or his representatives. Two instances will serve to indicate the general lines of this policy. In the first place, foremen and other supervisors are at present appointed and paid by the employer, and are often compelled to resign Trade Union membership, or at least active membership, on their appointment. Guildsmen desire that foremen and other direct supervisors of labour should be chosen (subject to qualifications for the post) by the workers, and that they should be members of the Trade Unions including these workers. Moreover, Guildsmen desire that such supervisors should be paid by the Union and not by the employer. Indeed, they desire that all workers should be in this position, the Union making a collective contract with the employer for the whole of the labour employed, and then paying the various individuals, including the supervisors, out of the sum received. This might operate either under a time-work, or under a collective piece-work system.

Secondly, Guildsmen lay great stress upon the development of workshop organisation as an integral part of Trade Union machinery. They see in the shop steward and the Trade Union Works Committee the germ of an organisation capable of assuming control of the productive processes in the workshop. They have therefore devoted considerable attention to the growth of this movement, and have endeavoured to bring out the importance of giving to it, as far as possible, a constructive character. At the same time, they have urged the importance of giving to workshop machinery a greater recognition and a more assured place in Trade Union organisation. In particular, they have emphasised the need for using workshop machinery as a means of fitting the Trade Unions for assuming the function of industrial management.

Of course, the greatest barrier to development on the lines suggested above is recognised by Guildsmen as lying in the present chaotic and sectional organisation of British Trade Unionism. They therefore advocate Industrial Unionism and the systematic amalgamation of Trade Unions on industrial lines. They recognise that it is impossible for the workers to assume any considerable measure of control while they are divided among a large number of sectional, and often competing or overlapping, Unions, so that in any particular establishment the workers employed often belong to as many as a dozen separate societies and sometimes to far more. A real policy of control clearly implies the unification of forces, and Guildsmen have therefore been prominent in the movement for amalgamation, and also for the organisation of the salariat in Trade Unions and, wherever possible, their fusion in one Society with the manual workers.

Some of the measures suggested above are directed primarily to the assumption of control in cases in which industries continue to be privately owned. Guildsmen, however, are opposed to private ownership of industry, and strongly in favour of public ownership. Of course, this does not mean that they desire to see industry bureaucratically administered by State departments. They aim at the control of industry by National Guilds including the whole personnel of the industry. But they do not desire the ownership of any industry by the workers employed in it. Their aim is to establish industrial democracy by placing the administration in the hands of the workers, but at the same time to eliminate profit by placing the ownership in the hands of the public. Thus the workers in a Guild will not be working for profit : the prices of their commodities and indirectly at least the level of their remuneration will be subject to a considerable measure of public control. The Guild system is one of industrial partnership between the workers and the public, and is thereby sharply distinguished from the proposals popularly described as " Syndicalist."

Immediately, Guildsmen press for the nationalisation or municipalisation of the ownership of every industry or service which can be regarded as ripe for public ownership, and especially of such great public sevices as mines, railways and other transport, shipbuilding and electricity. At the same time, in connection with any such measure of nationalisation, they aim at the immediate establishment of a form of workers' control, in order that the workers may at once assume the fullest share in the administration that is immediately practicable. Suggestions based upon this policy, as applied to some of the principal industries and services, are embodied in the subsequent chapters of this book. Their adoption would not, of course, mean the setting up of National Guilds ; but it would be a long step towards their creation.

I turn now to some of the morc theoretical aspects of the National Guilds system. As I explained at the outset, the governing idea of National Guilds is that of industrial self-government and democracy. Guildsmen hold that democratic principles are fully as applicable to industry as to politics : indeed, they feel that political institutions can never be really or fully democratic unless they are based on democratic institutions in the economic sphere. Their contention is that true democracy must really be functional democracy, in the sense that a democratic Commonwealth can only be based on the democratic organisation of all its parts. From the standpoint of the individual citizen this means that he should be self-governing in relation to the various functions which he performs—self-governing in his economic life as a producer or as a renderer of service to the community as well as in his capacity as a consumer or as a member of a national or local authority or of any other functional body.

I am fully conscious that this is a very inadequate explanation indeed ; but here I can hardly hope to do more than hint at the principles involved. For this book is not an account of National Guilds, but an attempt to apply Guild Socialist principles to the present economic situation. Perhaps I can make the point contained in the last paragraph, at least in those respect in which it is most directly relevant, clearer by putting it in another way. Industry and politics are at present mixed up together in a single great confusion. This is harmful to industry, to which political interference is at best a necessary evil ; and it is no less harmful to politics, which are constantly perverted from their true function by the intrusion of industrial considerations. Only by making each self-governing in its own sphere, while providing for their co-ordination in Society as a whole, can we hope to bring order out of chaos. Such a system of functional self-government is what Guildsmen seek. At the same time, they seek not merely autonomy in industry, but also democracy ; for, as long as there exist separate industrial classes whose interests in industry are opposed, self-government, in the sense of autonomy alone, will not work. A necessary basis for functional self-government is an approximate economic equality; for where warring classes exist they will not respect the territory of a separate function. Economic conflicts will overflow into the political field, and political conflicts into the economic field. Democratic self-government in industry and elsewhere, is therefore the key to the successful functioning of Society as an expression of the wills of its members.

CHAPTER V

COAL

I

THE COAL COMMISSION

COAL is the key industry of Great Britain in more senses than one. It forms the basis of production at home and of the export trade ; but it is even more important at the present time as the centre of the Labour struggle. The controversy which is now in progress in connection with the mining industry is in reality a controversy over the whole future basis of British industry. The point at issue is not only whether the coal mines are to be nationalised or not, but whether the principles of national ownership and democratic control are to be accepted as the principles which are applicable to the vital industries and services as a whole. That is why, although the immediate issue affects primarily the coal industry, the whole forces of both Capitalism and Labour are being gradually drawn into the conflict.

At the beginning of the year 1919, a serious crisis arose in the mining industry. The miners, who had been content during the war to wait for a more propitious time for advancing their demands, launched their National Programme, which included claims not only for reduced hours

nd higher wages, but also for the national ownership and
democratic control of the mining industry. For some time,
a national mining strike seemed to be imminent, and the
state of feeling in the country was at the time such that a
strike of the miners might well have precipitated a general
crisis and resulted in something like a general strike.
In these circumstances, the Government, while declaring
publicly that it would never yield to industrial pressure,
was exceedingly anxious to avert the strike, and proposed
a Royal Commission with powers to investigate and report
upon not only hours and wages, but the whole question of
the future ownership and control of the mining industry.
The miners at first were reluctant to fall in with this
scheme. They only did so when they were assured that,
apart from the Chairman, half the members of the Commission would be definitely Labour men, appointed or approved
by the Miners' Federation. Mr. Justice Sankey was appointed Chairman ; with him were three coal-owners, three
other employers, three miners and three " Labour intel-
ectuals," Messrs. Webb and Tawney, and Sir Leo Money.
The Commission sat in public, and its proceedings were
reported in the Press. The evidence given, with its widely
astonishing revelations of the wastefulness and inefficiency
of the system of private ownership, caused a sensation,
and did a great deal to convince the public of the justice
of the miners' claims. Two sets of Reports were issued,
the first dealing with hours and wages, and the second with
nationalisation. In the case of hours and wages, the
Government at once acted on the Report signed by the
Chairman and the three employers who were not coal-
owners, and gave the miners concessions which were substantial, although they still left a great deal to be desired.
The final Reports were four in number. The whole of the

members of the Commission pronounced in favour of th
nationalisation of mining royalties, and the Governmen
subsequently announced their intention of giving effec
to this policy. Apart from this, the three coal-owners an
two other employers signed a report which advocated th
retention of the present system without any importan
change. On the question of control, the horizon of thes
employers appeared to be limited to the proposals of th
Whitley Report. One Commissioner, Sir Arthur Duckham
favoured compulsory trustification of the coal industry
under private ownership, but with a limited participatio
by the workers in the control of the trusts. The Chairma
pronounced for national ownership with a small elemen
of workers' control, and the six Labour members for nationa
ownership with a much fuller element of control by th
workers.

The Coal Industry Commission thus resulted in a pro
nouncement by a majority of the members, includin
the eminent lawyer who was Chairman, in favour of th
nationalisation of coal mines and also of the concession t
the workers of a share in control. As soon as it became clea
that the volume and cumulative effect of the evidence i
favour of nationalisation could not be ignored—that is
long before the Commission had issued its Reports—th
capitalist interests directly affected determined to exert al
their strength in opposition. A temporary propagandis
body, the Coal Association, was called into being, an
received warm support from capitalists in other industries
especially among the iron and steel, engineering and ship
building magnates. Mr. Balfour, a member of the Com
mission, suddenly changed his mind. Having signed th
Chairman's Interim Report in favour of either nation
alisation or unification, he became convinced that th

present system must be maintained at all costs, and joined his fellow-employers in their final Report.   Sir Allan Smith, the chairman of the Engineering Employers' Federation, together with the cleverest of the mine-owners' leaders, Sir Adam Nimmo, was put on to the Commission after the first stage of the inquiry, and it became clear that there would be no compromise on the employers' side.

At the same time, the Coal Association launched its propagandist campaign.   Pamphlets, at most unremuneratively low prices, were issued, and were eagerly pushed by the big railway bookstalls which, in this country as elsewhere, show a marked preference for the literature of reaction.   In these pamphlets it was pointed out most clearly that the arguments in favour of nationalising the mines were for the most part equally applicable to other basic industries, and that the whole structure of capitalist industrialism was menaced by the threat to the " key " industry of mining.   Pamphlets, however, do not, as a rule, reach a very wide circle, and at the same time an enormous Press campaign was undertaken.   Space was bought at high rates throughout the provincial newspapers, and a swarm of articles directed against nationalisation began to appear in every newspaper which was willing to accept them.   Even coal merchants began to deliver leaflets denouncing nationalisation with the coal at their customers' doors.

The struggle was also waged in the political sphere, both openly in Parliament and still more fiercely behind the scenes.   The Parliament elected in 1918 being to all intents and purposes the " executive committee for administering the affairs of the whole capitalist class " anticipated in the Communist Manifesto, naturally threw itself, under orders from its real masters, wholeheartedly into the task

5

of demonstrating the impossibility of carrying out any programme of nationalisation in the teeth of its opposition. The first demonstration was directed against the ambiguous and tentative proposals of the Government's Ways and Communications Bill, which was supposed to foreshadow a policy of railway nationalisation. Every clause in the Bill which could conceivably have been used to further such a project was ruthlessly hacked about in order to prevent even the smallest element of nationalisation from being introduced ; and when the Government's Electricity Bill made its appearance before Parliament it was at once subjected to the same treatment, until both measures were successfully reduced to the form of control by the State acting under the advice of the " Big Business " interests. Again and again the Government surrendered to these assaults, and conceded to the business representatives the whole substance of what they asked.

Meanwhile, behind the scenes, every form of pressure was being applied to persuade the Government to declare roundly against nationalisation in all its forms. This, however, in face of the attitude of the miners and the railwaymen, the Government was at first unwilling to do openly ; and, whatever may have been said privately to the capitalist leaders, the Government for some time would say no more publicly than that it had not yet made up its mind. This was bad enough ; for the Government had definitely promised during the last General Election that it would nationalise the railways, and Mr. Lloyd George had only averted a national coal strike by a very definite understanding that he would accept the findings of the Coal Commission. It is, however, more than doubtful whether, even if it had wished to do so, the Government could have carried a proposal to nationalise either coal mines or railways through the present House of Commons.

The plain fact is that Mr. Lloyd George and his Government only retained power by delivering themselves, bound hand and foot, into the power of the " Big Business " interests, and that these interests had definitely made up their minds to fight. There was a constantly growing tendency in capitalist circles to say that the great struggle with Labour was bound to come, and that it had better come soon than later.

The attitude of uncertainty and indecision could not be kept up for long by the Government. The miners raised the question of the action which should be taken in order to enforce nationalisation at the Trades Union Congress of September 1919, and secured overwhelming support for their demand, with a firm promise that they would receive the united backing of the Labour movement. Accompanied by representatives from the Congress, they waited on the Prime Minister, and presented to him their demand. Mr. Lloyd George, who had at an earlier stage already pronounced tentatively against nationalisation and in favour of a scheme of "trustification " based on Sir Arthur Duckham's proposal, was driven to take a final decision. On behalf of the Government he again promised the nationalisation of mining royalties ; but he entirely refused to agree to nationalisation of mines, and was ready to concede even less than Sir Arthur Duckham to the demand for a share in control. The miners, asked by him whether they preferred the retention of the present system without change or the adoption of the measures proposed by the Government, replied without hesitation that they preferred things as they are, and that the Government scheme was, from their point of view, worse than useless.

Thus closed the second phase of the struggle. The first phase covered the period from the crisis which led to the appointment of the Coal Commision to the date of its Final Report. This ended with a pronouncement by a majority of the Commissioners in favour of nationalisation with a measure of workers' control. The second phase was the phase of capitalist intrigue, culminating in the definite refusal of the Government to embark on any policy of nationalisation.

Naturally, this challenge was not left unanswered. The answer is contained in the national propagandist campaign for national ownership and democratic control of the mines which is now being conducted by the united forces of the Miners' Federation, the Trades Union Congress, the Labour Party and the Co-operative Union. Perhaps, by the time this book appears, a definite issue will have been reached, and the third phase of the struggle brought to a conclusion. However this may be, the coal question has already become the " token " issue of the day. The huge strength of the Miners' Federation, by far the strongest Trade Union in the world, and the vital character of the industry affected, make the struggle significant far beyond its direct bearing on the economic and political situation. Upon it, both Capitalism and Labour seem bent on exerting their full strength. To mere nationalisation such violent objection might not have been taken, had it not been for two things—first, that the example once set would certainly be followed in other cases ; and secondly, that it was clear from the outset that the miners were not seeking and would not be content with mere bureaucratic nationalisation, but would insist on the concession of a real share in control. The contagious example of workers' control rouses far more fear in capitalist circles than the contagion of national ownership; for nationalisation, with the present Government, would certainly carry with it compensation on a generous scale, while any substantial concession of control menaces the whole structure of Capitalism, financial as well as industrial.

II

THE NATIONALISATION ISSUE

Every day since the Coal Commission presented its First Report has made it more clear that the battle is joined over the question of nationalisation.

For the antagonists in this struggle there is, if not in both cases the assurance of success, at least the joy of battle. But the rest of the population cannot so easily share in this joy. Those consumers of coal and other vital commodities who are neither large property-owners nor industrial workers impatient of the old industrial system, are apt to be a little mystified by the character and the dimensions of the struggle which is proceeding around them. They are inclined to say that provided they get coal cheap and plentiful, or railway travel facilities cheap and plentiful, they do not greatly care how these things are done, or whether it is private enterprise, or State Socialism, or Guild Socialism that does them. This doubtful and hesitant section of the population is capable of being turned, by arguments rational and irrational, either for or against nationalisation.

The present situation appears to many of these " mere consumers " in a very unfavourable light. It appears to them that the struggle over nationalisation is purely a struggle between two sections of " producers," and that

the interests of the consumer are being entirely over-
looked. This diagnosis of the situation possesses an
element of truth ; but it is none the less wrong. The
real struggle is not so much between the capitalist " producer " and the workman producer as between the pro-
perty-owner and the workman. It is not really two rival
methods of production that are contending for mastery,
but two rival systems of wealth-distribution. The very
propaganda which is conducted by the coal-owners and
their allies, as well as the tactics of the propertied interests
in the House of Commons, serves to make this very clear.
Although a word is said now and then of the consumer,
the main ground of the opponents of nationalisation in
the case of coal or railways is that if private enterprise
is attacked in one case the result will be to undermine
the whole system of private enterprise. The fear of this
is the cause of the widespread support given to the coal-
owners by capitalists in the other great industries. The
cry throughout the world of capital is that " property
is in danger." Nor is hostility removed by the fact that
there is every likelihood that nationalisation, if it comes,
will be accompanied by more than adequate, and even
more than generous, compensation. It is felt, and felt
rightly, that if private ownership and control of the vital
industries disappear, no system of compensation will
prevent a drastic readjustment of the claims to income
of the various members of the community. Reduced to
a *rentier*, the capitalist is not optimistic about his chances
of retaining his present share of the national income.

It is important to realise that these tactics of the
opponents of national ownership have the effect of shifting the issue away from the question of efficiency and
service to the consumer to that of the rights of property.

It is truly remarkable how little argument is being advanced to prove that private enterprise is more efficient than national ownership. Indeed, neither the admitted chaos of railway administration nor the facts about the economic waste involved in the private ownership of collieries admit of argument. The opponents of mine nationalisation are compelled to turn their backs upon the revelations of the Coal Commission and to search out some other issue on which to fight. They have found two cries to suit their purpose. To their own class, and to all property-owners, great and small, they cry out that property is in danger ; and to all and sundry they shout with one voice that nationalisation means bureaucracy and government by officials from Whitehall. I shall have more to say of this second cry a little later : here I want to concentrate upon the first. " Property is in danger " is an ill-chosen ground on which to ask for the sympathy and the support of the consumer ; for it offers no guarantee, indeed holds out no hope, of more efficient service in the future. The issue of nationalisation has been forced to the front by the fact that the workers are no longer prepared to acquiesce in the continuance of the present system, and that they are now strong enough to make its continuance for any long time impossible. The signal examples of waste and inefficiency which the Coal Commission has brought publicly to light have existed, for those who had eyes to see, these many years ; but it is the human revolt of Labour that has brought them clearly into view. The argument for coal (and also for railway) nationalisation is thus twofold. It has been shown that private enterprise is inefficient, and the Labour revolt has made impossible its continuance even at that low degree of efficiency which it has hitherto possessed. We may not know fully how national ownership will work out in practice ; we may admit that the admission of the workers by hand and brain to a real share in control will have to pass through the stage of experiment before a completely satisfactory adjustment can be reached ; but we are faced, and the consumer especially is faced, by the fact that the propertied interests which are opposing nationalisation offer no alternative to the present system. In standing for the protection at all costs of private property and private enterprise they are merely inviting the consumer to ensure a progressive development of inefficiency as the Labour revolt becomes more continuous and more pronounced.

There is, of course, the alternative scheme of Sir A. Duckham, which professes to aim at the elimination of waste without the assumption of national ownership. But this scheme, although it has received the official blessing of Mr. Lloyd George's Government, has been repudiated by the coal-owners and their supporters (even Mr. Balfour, who at first pronounced for nationalisation or unification and condemned the present system, having scurried back in the Final Report to rejoin his capitalist colleagues) as well as by the miners. In these circumstances, no one can now maintain that it offers any hope of a remedy for Labour unrest, and therefore of efficient service for the consumer and the community. Unification, indeed, only offers to the consumer the maximum danger of exploitation by a trust, and to the worker the minimum protection and assurance of fair treatment.

Nationalisation, in its relation to such vital services as mining, railways and electricity, is destined to be the leading domestic issue of the near future. Already, elections are being fought about it, and a great deal of the time of

Parliament is being expended in capitalist demonstrations in force designed to bring pressure to bear upon the Government. Everything possible, from the imposition from transparent political motives of a 6s. increase in coal prices to a no less political threat to cut off holiday trains, has been done to prejudice the case of Labour in the eyes of the public. But before making up his mind against nationalisation of either coal, or railways, or electricity, each citizen ought to try to find the true answer to two fundamental questions : Is the continuance of private ownership compatible with the elimination of huge avoidable waste in production ? And is there any chance, under private ownership, of satisfying the legitimate aspirations of Labour, or of giving to the workers that sense of working for the community which is essential if smooth operation in industry is to be possible ? A negative answer to these two questions does not, of course, prove that public ownership will provide a complete and final remedy. But is there in any other course even the remote possibility of a remedy ? And, if there is not, must we not give public ownership a trial ?

With a Government unwilling to nationalise or to grant any real democratic control in industry, with a Parliament which would probably refuse to follow the Government if it did decide in favour of nationalisation, and with the powerful industrial forces of the Triple Alliance determined to secure national ownership and democratic control, it seems almost inevitable that there will come a tremendous economic struggle. Its coming may be put off again and again : strikes like the big strikes which have already taken place may recur and be again settled ; but these postponements and partial settlements cannot have abiding results. It is a choice between great experiments in socially controlled industry and a gigantic industrial upheaval—either a strike or a lock-out, according as the one side or the other finally decides to precipitate the conflict. A dissolution, followed by the election of a new Parliament of different temper, might give the crisis a political as well as an industrial form, but I incline to the opinion that the industrial struggle will take place, and that the main issue will be that of national ownership and democratic control, first of the coal industry, and secondarily of vital industries in general.

It is by no means a comfortable situation for such a country as Great Britain, which has been so used to smooth-running industrial prosperity in the commercial sense as to regard it as a prescriptive British right. But it is slowly being realised that Britain's position as the spoilt child of Capitalism is largely gone, and that " reconstruction " must mean for us something very different from a mere return to pre-war conditions. Whether we shall accomplish " reconstruction " without a violent upheaval, it is impossible to say with certainty. I do not believe in a coming British " revolution " in the ordinary sense unless it be a revolution forced upon Labour by a panic-stricken and therefore bullying capitalist class ; but I do believe that the situation in the coal industry alone will be enough to lead before long to a bitter, and possibly prolonged, industrial conflict. Whichever side wins in this actual conflict, public ownership seems inevitable. Whether they win or lose, the miners cannot be made to render effective service again under Capitalism ; and, if for the sake of the consumer alone, this fact will necessarily lead, sooner or later, to the trial of the system of public ownership. This in turn, and for the same reason, will have to be combined with experiments in democratic control ; for the twofold problem of efficiency cannot be solved unless both the material and the human factors are taken fully into account. Material efficiency necessitates unification ; and this in turn, because of the menace of a huge capitalistic trust, necessitates national ownership. But equally the human claims of the miner make necessary not only national-isation, in order that private profit may be eliminated from the industry, but also democratic control, in order that the spirit of service may find room for free expression.

Nor will it be possible for long to confine these changes to a single industry. Their example will be contagious, and no attempts to discredit their financial results will prevent the contagion. Capitalism, even if it succeeds in defeating Labour for the moment in the coming struggle, will find its victory barren because no economic or political power on earth can draw efficient profit-making service from large bodies of men who are both strongly organised and con-vinced that the conditions under which they are working are anti-social and inefficient. Private ownership in the coal-mines and in other vital industries is doomed : it remains to be seen whether Labour is as powerful to con-struct as to destroy. Our estimate of the chances must depend on an examination of the constructive forces which are at work in British Labour, and especially of the con-structive programme which the coal-miners urged with such force and persuasiveness upon the Coal Commission and the public.

III

The Miners' Scheme

What, then, do the miners suggest as the way out of the coal crisis ? The public cannot complain that the proposals of the Miners' Federation have not been placed before them in a clear and detailed form. Before the Coal Industry Commission, the miners' witnesses, backed up by others, presented a fully drafted scheme, based on the national ownership of the mining industry and on the full participation of the workers in its control at every stage. This scheme embraced the whole of the problems involved, from the compensation to be paid to the coal-owners to the method of distribution to be adopted. One of the most important features, from the consumer's standpoint, was the proposal that the distributions of coal for household use should pass entirely into the hands of the Local Authorities and Co-operative Societies.

I desire here, however, to deal exclusively with that part of the scheme which is concerned with the control of the mines under national ownership. It is of the greatest importance that both the general intention behind this scheme and the detailed proposals contained in it should be clearly understood by the public. It is essential to disentangle the new Guild Socialist proposal made by the miners from Syndicalism on the one hand, and from State Socialism on the other.

The essence of the proposals lies in the entrusting of the management of the mining industry to a system of Councils on which the various grades of mine-workers will be represented. In the first place, it is proposed that the central administration should be entrusted to a National Mining Council, and that half the members of this Council should be chosen by the Miners' Federation of Great Britain. Secondly, it is proposed that there should be in each coal-field a District Council, and that half the members of each District Council should be chosen by the District Miners' Association. Thirdly, Pit

Committees are proposed, and half of their members are
to be chosen by the organised workers in the pit concerned.

So far the scheme is perfectly clear. But at once the
question arises, Who is to choose the remaining half of the
members of these various Councils and Committees? In
the case of the National Council, the scheme lays down
that the other half shall be chosen by the State.

What manner of persons, then, are these nominees of
the State intended to be? Are they to be politicians, or
ordinary Civil Servants, or representatives of the consumers,
or experts, or something else, or a hotch-potch of all
these various classes? I think the intention of the scheme
is clear, and although it is not directly stated in the scheme
itself, it was fully brought out in some of the evidence.
It is that the "other half" of the National Council should
be chosen to represent the various grades and types of
managers and experts who are no less essential to the
efficient conduct of the mining industry than the manual
workers themselves. The miners, as Mr. Hodges' recent
speeches amply show, recognise to the full the place of
the manager and the expert in industrial control, and are
prepared to accord to them their due position as partners
with the manual workers in the control of the enterprise.

These technical and managerial grades—managers,
under-managers, colliery engineers and other experts—
are not at present organised together with the manual
workers in a single organisation, nor have they as yet
recognised in the mass their community of interest with
the manual workers. The miners, therefore, cannot
legislate for them directly: they can at most only make
them a full and frank offer of partnership in control.
There is, among the younger men in these grades, an un-
doubted drift towards Trade Unionism and towards the

idea of a close alliance with the manual workers ; and it is upon this tendency that the miners' scheme is acting as a powerful stimulant. The very possibility of the smooth and fully efficient working of the miners' scheme depends upon a close alliance between the manual workers and the technical and managerial grades.

The idea, then, behind the miners' proposal is that the "other half" on the various Councils should be chosen from the technical and managerial grades. If these grades will accept an alliance with the miners, their respective organisations can undertake the task of nominating their representatives upon the Councils, and the need for nomination by the State will disappear. There is, however, a very serious obstacle to the consummation of this alliance at the present stage. This obstacle is not, as many outsiders will probably imagine, the unwillingness of the miners to recognise the management, or of the management to co-operate with their "social inferiors." Both these obstacles exist to a steadily diminishing extent. The real obstacle is simply the *fear* of the managerial grades that, if they show any sign of a willingness to ally themselves with the miners, they will be dismissed, black-listed, victimised and refused all chance of promotion. Their organisation is by no means so strong and cohesive as that of the miners ; and, being comparatively few in number, they are now more susceptible to individual intimidation than the strongly combined manual workers. Even if social prejudice and fear that the miners will not recognise their distinctive position and responsibilities count for something, fear of the mine-owners counts for much more. I fully believe that, if the miners could give a firm undertaking that national ownership and democratic control based on partnership would be at once enforced, they could enlist the immediate support of most of the younger elements in the managerial grades.

In suggesting that the " other half " on the Councils should be representative of the technicians and managers, I do not mean to suggest that all of these can be simply chosen, in the same way as the miners' representatives, by associations integral to the structure of the mining industry. The representatives of mine managers, under-managers and mining engineers could be so chosen ; but the technique of coal production and distribution demands the presence of other experts who could not be chosen in quite the same way. A geological expert, a traffic expert, a coal conservation expert, a person thoroughly equipped to deal with the export trade, would also be necessary. These other experts might be chosen by the State, although I myself believe that it would be better for them to be chosen by the Mining Council itself, in consultation, where possible, with any technical associa-tion concerned. In any case, it is not proposed that the State should choose any of the members of the District Councils or Pit Committees, the experts upon these being chosen under the scheme by the National or District Councils respectively. If the national managerial and technical associations chose their own representatives upon the National Mining Council, it would also follow that the corresponding district associations would choose their representatives upon the District Councils.

So far, I have been describing what the miners' scheme, as I understand it, involves, without entering into its merits from the public point of view. It is now time to endeavour to meet certain objections which are certain to be raised. Probably the first of these will be, " Why are not the consumers to be represented on the Mining Councils ? "

Before we begin to argue about this point, let us be clear what the functions of the Councils will be. They will be not advisory or deliberative, but actual managing and executive bodies. This being so, it is necessary that they should be staffed by the persons who know best how to manage and administer. So far from the consumers gaining from direct representation upon them, I believe they would lose ; for it is certainly to the consumers' interest that the mining industry should be conducted with the highest possible degree of technical efficiency. The consumer requires most certainly safeguards which will secure that the industry is conducted in the public interest ; but he requires also the fullest industrial efficiency. If the safeguards can be provided by means other than representation upon the management, he will do far better to leave the administration in the hands of those who understand the industry, and to get his safeguards by these other means.

There are two reasons why a joint body of producers and consumers is not likely to be an efficient instrument *for the actual management of industry*. The first is that the consumer, as a non-expert among experts, is more likely on detailed points of administration to confuse the issue and decrease the efficiency of the service than really to serve the interests of those whom he represents. The second reason, which is intimately connected with the first, is that the chief hope of really efficient public service lies in placing each industry " upon its honour," and in throwing directly and fully upon it the responsibility for the efficient conduct of the industry as a public service. Any complaint which the consumer has to make, and any point of view which he desires to state, will carry far more weight if he puts them as an external critic rather than as a member of a managing body on which his in-expert voice will be easily overborne by the force of expert opinion. Ways and means are the business of the industry itself : ends are that of the consumers and of the whole community.

What, then, is the alternative method by which, under the miners' scheme, the consumers would be able to express their desires and to make their complaints. The miners propose the constitution of a Consumers' Council representing the various classes of coal users, household, municipal, industrial, bunker, export and the rest. This Council, they suggest, should be, for the present at least, advisory and not executive ; but it should meet both separately and in joint session with the Mining Council, and should have full power to make complaints and offer suggestions as to the conduct of the industry. Similarly, there would need to be District Coal Consumers' Councils, meeting and dealing with the District Mining Councils.

But what, it will be asked, is to happen if the Mining Council refuses to pay any attention to the claims of the consumers ? The consumers have then two remedies. The first, and very powerful remedy, is that of publicity, based on full access to the books and transactions of the whole mining industry. The second remedy is that of an appeal to the State, ensured by the direct access of the Coal Consumers' Council to Parliament. This remedy may not be of great value to the public with such a Parliament as now exists, but if Parliament is to be recognised at all as a representative national authority in industrial matters, it must clearly be the consumers' court of appeal. This would be greatly facilitated if Parliament reformed

6

its organisation, and constituted a special committee to which the consumers' case could be brought, this Committee representing the State in its capacity as owner.

I am far from suggesting that this form of organisation is finally or completely satisfactory ; but I do believe that it gives the consumers the best chance of an effective voice that they can secure without a complete *bouleverse-ment* of the present social and political system, which is an eventuality I am not at present discussing. At a later stage, it may be that the Coal Consumers' Council will itself be recognised as the representative of the public in relation to the control of the industry and will acquire far more than advisory powers. But there is one very good reason why it cannot be given such a status at the present time. Much coal passes not to public bodies or individual consumers, but to capitalist concerns for use in further production or in distribution. These capitalist interests, while they continue to exist, will have to be represented on the Coal Consumers' Council, side by side with the representatives of household consumers and public bodies. But the objections to conferring public powers on a body partly representative of capitalist associations are overwhelming. This, and not any desire to restrict the rights of the consumers, is the reason why, while capitalism exists, any Consumers' Council can be only advisory.[1]

It must be borne in mind throughout that the whole scheme put forward by the miners is based and depends absolutely upon the national ownership of the mining industry. The Miners' Federation has summarily rejected the Govern-

[1] It will be necessary to insist that not only the capitalists in the industries which use coal, but also the workers employed in these industries, are represented on the Consumers' Councils The workers in the steel industry are just as much concerned with the efficiency of the mining industry as the steel employers.

ment's proposal to confer a measure of control upon the workers while retaining private capitalist ownership of the industry. They have done this because they feel that democratic control cannot effectively coexist with private profit. Their attitude is supported by that of the mine-owners, who have given the clearest possible expression to their view that private ownership cannot effectively coexist with democratic control, and have stated that they would prefer nationalisation. Thus, we find owners and workers agreeing that the combination of their rival points of view into a single scheme is utterly impracticable.

In considering, therefore, the position of the consumers under the miners' scheme we must always remember that the industry is to be nationally owned, and that, behind the Consumers' Council, the consumers have a second line of defence in the State. What exactly does this imply? It means that the mine-workers who are placed in control of their industry will be working it, not for any one's profit, but as a recognised part of the whole national economy. Take the three closely related questions of prices, remuneration and surplus as illustrations of the position which will arise under such a scheme. The final control of price is not a matter which the community can afford to leave the workers in a particular industry to decide for themselves. But neither is the final determination of price a power which is in any way essential to the democratic control of industry. Price is a social and not a purely industrial question.

While, therefore, the actual issuing of prices may rest with the Mining Council, not only will the Consumers' Council have the power of making public representations as to price, but also, if it cannot secure satisfaction directly, of appealing to the State to limit or regulate prices. In a developed

Guild Society, a better mechanism for dealing with prices will no doubt be devised ; but, for the present, the miners' scheme would leave the final control of coal prices with the State, acting probably through the special House of Commons Committee mentioned above.

Neither can the producers have the final word as to the general level of remuneration in any particular industry. Here, again, the actual issuing of schedules of rates will, no doubt, rest with the Mining Council ; but a similar power of making public representations will belong to the consumers, and any proposal to vary wage-rates will have to receive the endorsement of the State. Doubtless, the economic power of the organised miners will count for something in determining rates ; but is there any system possible at present under which this will not be the case ?

Thirdly, the consumer has the final safeguard that any surplus realised by the working of the mines will belong, not to the miners, but to the whole community.   It will pass into the National Exchequer, and if, as may be hoped, some of it is earmarked for capital development in the mines, it will in that case rank with the national capital already sunk in the mining industry.   Whether it produces revenue or not will depend on the policy adopted by the community in either treating the mining industry as a revenue-producing department or cheapening the cost of living and of production in other industries by selling coal at cost price.

In short, the miners' scheme amply safeguards both the consumer and the communal interest.   It gives a better chance of efficient mining development than any other scheme in the field, and it deserves the support of the consumer fully as much as that of the producer.   This is on its productive side ; but it has also the advantage that upon it, far more easily than upon any other system, could be based an efficient scheme of public coal distribution free from every taint of private profit.   With this aspect of it I shall deal separately in discussing the problem of distribution as a whole.[1]

[1] See Chapter X, esp. p. 200.

CHAPTER VI

RAILWAYS

I

The Pivot of Reconstruction

MOST people thought in December, 1918, that the future of the railways was settled. It was supposed that when Mr. Churchill definitely stated during the General Election that the Government had decided to nationalise the railways, he was speaking, as Mr. Thomas might say, " with a full sense of his responsibility." No member of the Government took occasion to contradict his statement, and it was generally assumed that he had spoken with the authority of the War Cabinet behind him. There was even a slight upward movement of railway shares on the strength of his announcement. Subsequent events, however, soon indicated that Mr. Churchill was expressing not the adopted policy of the Government, but merely his own " humble opinion." For when the National Union of Railwaymen went to interview the Prime Minister on the subject of railway nationalisation in the following month, they were blandly informed that the whole question was " held over for the present."

Where, then, do we stand ? It is abundantly clear that upon the future of our transport system very many of the principal problems of reconstruction depend. Housing furnishes an obvious example. Local authorities are now being urged to press on immediately with housing schemes designed to meet the serious shortage caused by the war. Can they do this intelligently or well until they know what transport facilities will be available ? There is a growing public opinion in favour of basing our post-war housing policy as far as possible upon the principle of decentralisation. Our towns are overgrown, and it is widely held that now, when a vast number of new houses must be built, is the time to tackle the whole question of urban and rural development. Not merely town-planning on limited sites, not merely suburban extensions of our monstrous and dropsical cities, but the conscious development of new towns and villages, and even more the re-creation and re-vitalising of existing small towns, should be the aims of our housing policy at the present time. This policy could, indeed, only be fully realised if the whole question were being dealt with from a national standpoint by a department very different in outlook from the present Ministry of Health, and locally by authorities very different in spirit from most of the existing local Councils ; but even with these drawbacks much could be done if there were an assurance that the necessary transport facilities would be available.

The breaking-up of our huge towns, the destruction of slum areas and brick-box monstrosities, and with these things the eradication of many forms of vice and disease which are the direct products of environment, are all matters which depend in a very real sense upon the character and control of our transport system. We cannot house our population under pleasant, healthy or beautiful conditions ; we can indeed only intensify the existing problems of urban concentration and overcrowding, until we determine to provide new transport facilities on a scale and of a kind which are utterly beyond the reach of private enterprise.

The housing of the people is not, of course, an isolated or self-contained problem. Under modern conditions we have for the most part to live in close proximity to the centres in which industries and businesses are congregated. Even if we built the most beautiful and healthful new towns, most people could not go and live in them unless there were factories and workshops at hand to afford employment. Now, factories and workshops are dependent, to an ever-increasing extent, upon transport facilities. They must receive, often from long distances, their coal, their raw materials and their plant, and they must have convenient means at hand for the dispatch of the commodities which they produce. The people can only move into the country if the factories move, and the factories cannot move unless the facilities for transport are provided.

Moreover, there is a further complication. Just as the workers cannot move until the factories move, so the factories cannot move until there are houses for the workers to live in. The supply of labour is a vital consideration for the modern employer, and he frequently keeps his works in the big towns, where rents are high, merely because he is there assured of an abundant supply of workers.

In short, Reconstruction in housing and in industry alike —to say nothing of health and happiness—depends very largely upon the way in which we deal with the transport problem.

What has been said is enough to show that the adoption of a clear and definite transport policy is an immediate as well as a vital necessity. It would not, however, be enough even if the Government at once made up its mind to proceed with railway nationalisation. Even if we leave aside the question of shipping, which is vital from an international as well as a national point of view, the whole problem of internal transport clearly hangs together. What is required is not merely the nationalisation of the railways and the extension of railway facilities, but the development of a national system co-ordinating the various forms of internal transport.

The very idea of a national transport system, especially when it is presented as the pivot, so to speak, of a national system of serial Reconstruction, is one which many minds simply refuse to entertain. Each separate problem—the railway problem, the tramway problem, the canal problem, the motor problem, the shipping problem and the air problem—seems by itself too large to be properly handled on traditional lines, and it is feared that the running together of several problems will merely increase the complication. But is this really true ? Is it not rather the case that the various branches of internal transport at least must be treated as a whole, and have their places assigned to them within a general scheme designed to suit new conditions ?

Let us attempt a brief survey of the situation. The continuance of the war-time control of the railways is obviously ineffective, both because it provides no motive for railway development, and because it leaves almost intact the sectionalism and self-centred administration of the separate lines. It does not even link up the present railways into a coherent system ; and still less does it provide for the building of new lines and the full development of existing facilities, especially in the rural districts. It is, in fact, open to exactly the same objections as the continuance of the pre-war system of private control.

Moreover, as long as the railways are privately owned, the canals will be largely immobilised, and there can be no real attempt to develop the canals as carriers of heavy goods where cheapness is more important than rapidity of transit. Again, it is almost impossible, as well as undesirable, to conceive of the railways, under private or under indirect State control, taking full advantage of the enormous possibilities presented by commercial road transport by motor, especially for short-distance transit. If, for the moment, we look at the transport problem purely from the side of goods transport, there is clearly an overwhelming case for the co-ordination of inland transport by rail, water and road into a single system, coherently organised and developed by a single authority. In such a field the public itself has no possible competitor except a monopolistic organisation whose power would be too huge for the public even to contemplate permitting it to exist.

On the side of passenger transport the case is no less clear, even if it is more complicated, because local authorities and local companies deal, to a great extent, with traffic by tram or omnibus. This fact, however, does not lessen the need for national co-ordination, and the obvious inadequacy of many municipal areas to permit of the development of reasonable systems of local transport presents a clear case for national action directed to encouraging local control over wider areas. Clearly the proposed scheme for a small number of huge centralised power-stations for the whole country is closely bound up with the future of local electric traction, whether by tram or by rail.

The case is overwhelming for a real Ministry of Transport, based upon public ownership of the railways and canals, but also actively engaging in road transport and vigorously promoting the development of new railways, light railways and canals, and also actively supervising and co-ordinating the local transport facilities provided by other bodies, and endeavouring to bring local transport areas more into harmony with local and national needs. It is clear that the Government's policy of " holding over for the present " the larger questions of reorganisation is not merely foolish in itself, but likely to be fatal to our hopes of real reconstruction in other spheres. If the delay is prolonged, and unless a national transport system is promptly set on foot, we may build houses and factories, but we shall build them in the wrong places ; we may settle soldiers on the land, but they will be most unlikely to stop there ; we may have established a Ministry of Health, but we shall not succeed in raising the national standard of health ; we may even get in the long run slightly better transport facilities, but with them will probably go the dangers and disadvantages of private monopoly. It is to the interest of every section in the community—trader and traveller, employer and workman, industrialist and agriculturalist, doctor and teacher—that transport facilities should be free and abundant, and coherently planned from a national point of view. In a very real sense, the transport problem is the pivot of reconstruction, and by the Government's handling of it we may begin to judge of their intentions in other spheres. So far, we know only that the Ministry of Transport is contenting itself with minor patchings-up of the old system, and that all larger projects of development are " held over for the present."

II

THE PLUMB PLAN

National ownership of the railway and allied transport services, we have seen, is essential, not only because it is the condition of efficiency in these services themselves, but also because it is the condition of efficiency in many other spheres of social action. But, as in the case of the mining industry, national ownership is only half the problem ; for we shall be most unlikely to get the smooth working and comprehensive development which are required, if national ownership is to carry with it bureaucratic control. We must therefore discuss not only the ownership of the transport services, but also the form of management and control to be adopted when they pass under public ownership.

Before we begin to discuss the present railway situation in this country from this point of view, it will be well to describe briefly the movement for public ownership and democratic control of the railroads which has grown up in the United States under the name of the " Plumb Plan."

What is the " Plumb Plan " ? is a question that is beginning to be widely asked, in Labour circles at least, in this country.

The answer is that it is a project for national ownership and joint control of the American railroads, first put forward by the American railroad Trade Unions at the beginning of the year 1919, and widely advocated throughout the United States as the only hopeful solution of the railroad problem. British workers in the mines and on the railways, who are themselves putting forward projects of national ownership and joint control, certainly

ought to know about the plan which is being advocated by
their comrades across the water.

Why is it called the " Plumb Plan " ? Because it was
formulated by the railroad Trade Unions on the advice of
Mr. Glenn E. Plumb, who has been for some years their
legal adviser and counsel. In America, as in this country,
workers by hand and brain are collaborating in devising
schemes for the future control of industry. Mr. Plumb
has co-operated with the railroad workers, as Messrs.
Tawney and Webb, Sir Leo Money and others collaborated
with our miners on the Coal Commission.

The *Plumb Plan League* is an *ad hoc* organisation created
by the railway Trade Unions of America to advocate the
taking over of the railroads by the State, and their control
on democratic lines. It is at present conducting a vigorous
propaganda through pamphlets and leaflets, to say nothing
of a weekly journal. It has produced, like our own
miners, a Bill designed to give full effect to its scheme ;
and this Bill has been submitted to the United States
Senate. It is from this Bill and from its pamphlets that
the following details of the scheme are taken. The miners,
through the United Mine Workers' Association of America,
have endorsed the " Plan," and have recently pledged their
full support to the railwaymen ; but their plans are not
so far advanced, and the details of the Bill which they are
preparing are not yet known.

Taken as a whole, the "Plumb Plan," with a few important
differences, bears a remarkable resemblance to the schemes
put forward by Guild Socialists in this country and largely
adopted by the Miners' Federation in the scheme described
in the last chapter. It provides, in the first place, for
the buying out of all private interests in the railroads
and the complete and permanent assumption of ownership

by the public. It is proposed that all private railroad interests should be eliminated by the issue to them of Government bonds in return for their *real capital*, not including water or other forms of fictitious capital. The purchase of the railroads is to be supervised by a Purchasing Board, on which the Government and the workers and the railroad managers will be represented.

With national ownership is to go joint control. The " Plumb Plan " is anti-bureaucratic, and does not propose that the railroads should be managed by the State. It suggests a board of fifteen directors, of whom one-third will be nominated by the Government, one-third by the managerial staff and one-third by the manual workers. It is thus based on a sharing of control between three parties—the organised " rank and file " railroad workers, the managerial grades and the public. It advocates the establishment of a central Railroad Commission equally representing these three parties, the representatives of the " rank and file " workers and of the management being directly chosen by those whom they are to represent, and the representatives of the public being appointed by the President of the United States. The body thus constituted is to be an actual managing and controlling authority, entrusted with the task of running the railroads on behalf of the public. This is, of course, generally in conformity with the British miners' proposal, and is very different from the purely Advisory Council contemplated in Sir John Sankey's Report.

The managing body, however, is not to have absolutely unfettered control. The rates charged by the railroads are, it is recognised, a matter of such general public concern that they cannot be left to be determined at will by a Council predominantly representative of the industry. It is therefore proposed that maximum rates for freightage and passenger traffic shall be fixed on behalf of the public by the inter-State Commerce Commission, whose consent would be required for any raising of freights. Here the American scheme is confronted with exactly the same difficulty as the mining scheme described in the last chapter. The desirability of final public control over prices is recognised ; but the British House of Commons and the American Congress are alike mainly capitalistic in character, and will therefore be much more likely to look after the interests of the capitalist than after those of the consumer. In default, however, of any body really representing the public, both American and British Labour are driven back upon very second-rate substitutes. This, however, is inevitable in the early stages of reorganisation under a still predominantly capitalist society.

The " Plumb Plan " makes provision not only for the central organisation, but also for devolution. The proposed regional and local government of the industry follows the same lines as the central control, with regional Councils consisting of the same three elements acting under the direction of the central Council. Here, again, the American plan follows the same line as that of the British miners.

The principal divergence appears, it is not surprising to find, in the proposed method of dealing with the surplus earnings of the industry after salaries and running expenses have been paid. This surplus, it is proposed, should normally be divided into two equal parts, of which one would go to the State for wiping off the debt on the railroads and providing for new capital expenditure. It is interesting to note that it is proposed that a proportion of new capital expenditure for opening fresh routes should be borne by the territories served by such routes. The other half of the surplus is to be divided among the workers by hand and brain in proportion to their earnings, with this difference, that each managerial worker is to receive twice as much, in proportion to his earnings, as each "rank and file" worker. Thus, if the "rank and file" workers receive out of the surplus 5 per cent on their earnings, the managerial workers will receive 10 per cent. The purpose of this disparity is explained as being the necessity of making the rewards and incentives of management commensurate with the responsibility.

The surplus which will be thus distributed is to be limited. If the total surplus amounts to 10 per cent or more of the gross revenue of the railways, it is provided that railway rates must be reduced by 5 per cent, or by half of any larger percentage of surplus. It is estimated that reduced rates will bring more business, and that this will mean a reduction in costs, and bring the surplus up to its old figure, when a further reduction in rates will follow.

This is a very broad outline of the "Plumb Plan." Some of its features are obviously "American," and arise directly out of the economic and psychological conditions of American industry. No one supposes or desires that anything exactly like the "Plumb Plan" will be advocated or adopted in this country; but clearly the general outline closely resembles, except in the provisions for giving Labour and Management a share in the surplus, the schemes which are being advocated by miners and railway workers in this country. The demand for control made so strongly by a body of American Trade Unions supposed to be eminently conservative is especially interesting; for we are always told to regard America as the strongest and least menaced of the strongholds of capitalism. Yet here we find Mr. Gompers, who is now beginning to move leftwards under pressure from his own " rank and file," acting as president of the " Plumb Plan League."

Personally, I believe that the scheme of national ownership and joint control put before the Coal Commission by Mr. Straker on behalf of the Miners' Federation is a much better scheme than the " Plumb Plan." It provides for the joint control of industry by the workers " by hand and brain," and it does this without including any element of profit-sharing, even in a modified form.

The scheme proposed by the " Plumb Plan League " may be right for the United States ; but I do not believe that this feature of it is right for us. It is, of course, only fair to distinguish the proposal to divide the surplus very sharply from any ordinary proposal of profit-sharing ; for the only surplus concerned is one which results directly from improved efficiency and lowered costs of railroad operation. Probably, the presence of such a feature is not enough to merit the rejection of the scheme as a whole. Far more definite is the objection to the double rate of bonus proposed for the managerial grades, which would mean that these grades would benefit out of proportion to the difference between their salaries and those of the manual workers. It ought to be recognised that improved efficiency of service depends no less upon the willing co-operation of the manual workers than upon the ability and initiative of the managerial grades.

There can be no doubt that the " Plumb Plan " has a considerable momentum behind it. It has the backing not only of all the powerful Railroad Brotherhoods and other Railroad Unions, but of the American Federation of Labour as a whole. It is at present at the stage of extremely efficient and thorough propaganda, and no question of taking immediate " direct action " to enforce it has

yet come under consideration ; for, although it emerged
in the course of the recent strikes in the American railroad
workshops, these strikes actually centred round quite
different issues. The present intention of the Railroad
Brotherhoods and of the League appears to be that of first
appealing to the public by propaganda activity to the
fullest possible extent, and then of making the railroad
question an issue as far as they can in the forthcoming
Presidential Election. Only if these methods fail is it at
present intended to discuss the question of direct action.

The position which has led to the "Plumb Plan" becoming
an important and immediate issue in America is very much
the same as the position which has forced similar questions
to the front both in this country and in Germany. State
control of mines and railways will be variously estimated
as having succeeded or failed by persons of different
opinions ; but there can be no question of its indefinite
continuance in its present form. The return of normal
conditions will compel us to go forward to national ownership, or else to go back and give up the control of railways
which has been developed under abnormal conditions.
Going back, in most cases, involves a double difficulty. In
the first place, the reversion to private control is in most
cases only possible if freights are allowed to remain permanently at a level which the public will hardly tolerate
as a permanent institution. Secondly, it is more than
doubtful whether, in the industries concerned, the workers
can ever be persuaded again to work, or at least to give
of their best, under private ownership or for private
profit.

It is the second difficulty, which is by far the more serious,
that is forcing upon the consideration of the public the
schemes of ownership and control devised or adopted and

put forward by the workers themselves. They have to be considered, because the failure or refusal of Labour to give good service under private ownership or without a real measure of control would be by itself fatal to the prospects of industrial efficiency and reasonable public service.

In one respect at least recent events seem to show that the workers in America are behaving with greater wisdom and foresight than their compeers in Great Britain. The activities of the " Plumb Plan League " are evidence that the American Trade Unions realise the importance of public opinion, and that they are prepared to expend money and energy upon propaganda designed to influence it. That is one of the reasons why it is important that British Trade Unionists should know about the "Plumb Plan," and, in particular, that our own railwaymen should take a lesson from the American Trade Unions in the matter of propaganda.

The miners, first with the aid of the Labour Research Department, and later jointly with the national bodies representing the whole Labour movement, have done some effective work towards educating the public up to the ideas of nationalisation with workers' control, and are intending to do more.

The railwaymen, on the other hand, have so far done practically nothing either to prepare a definite scheme or to put their case before the public. Yet this is most urgently required. The public still confuses public ownership with bureaucracy, and has hardly yet begun to realise that what the workers want is neither State management nor Syndicalism, but control by the workers by hand and brain in conjunction with the public. The Guild Socialists have been pushing that idea for some years ; but now that it has become the accepted policy of our great Trade Unions, the propaganda ought to be greatly intensified, and the Unions themselves ought to take the first place in conducting it.

The solution of national ownership with workers' control is the only solution of the transport problem ; for the workers will no longer be content to work either for the profit of capitalists or without self-government in industry for themselves. It is only a question whether this will come violently or through a gradual change. If it is agreed that violence should be avoided if possible, let us get on with the propaganda. We have the example of the workers in European countries to hearten us in the task ; and now at last the " Plumb Plan " shows that America is moving in the same direction. The railway workers of the world are uniting to demand national ownership and democratic control of their industry.

III

CONTROL ON THE RAILWAYS

The railway workers are now exceedingly well organised. The National Union of Railwaymen includes in its 450,000 members the vast majority of the manual workers in the traffic grades, except in the locomotive sections. These are equally well organised, but are divided between the N.U.R. and the Associated Society of Locomotive Engineers and Firemen, which has about 40,000 members, belonging entirely to the locomotive grades. In the railway locomotive and other construction and repair shops, the N.U.R. divides the membership with a large number of craft Unions belonging chiefly to the engineering and woodworking trades. The general labour Unions have some members in the shops, but most of the

less skilled shopmen are in the N.U.R., while the skilled
workers are divided in their allegiance. The N.U.R.
also includes a few thousand supervisory workers,
including some inspectors and stationmasters ; but the
majority of the supervisory grades, almost to the top of the
service, are organised, together with practically all the
clerical workers, in the Railway Clerks' Association,
which has a membership of about 90,000. If we allow a
maximum of 50,000 for the craft and general labour
Unions, this gives a total of nearly 650,000 organised
railway employees, out of a total of about 725,000 employed
by the railway companies.

The position therefore seems to be even more favourable
in the railway service than in the mining industry for the
immediate adoption of an effective scheme of democratic
control. For the difficulty of securing the full co-operation
of the managerial and technical grades is very much less
in consequence of the fact that the majority of these grades
have already thrown in their lot with the Trade Union
Movement. This is not to say that no difficulty exists ;
for a great deal remains to be done before full co-operation,
in fact and in spirit, can be established between the manual
workers and the supervisory grades. The situation, however, is already promising ; for all three railway Unions
stand definitely for the principle of control, and, if they
could be brought together to formulate an agreed scheme,
the requisite solidarity ought easily to follow upon its
presentation.

Unfortunately, this has not yet been done. The R.C.A.
scheme was drawn up, so far as is known, without consultation with the N.U.R. and the Associated Society,
while the N.U.R. is believed to have put forward its
demands to the Government in conjunction with the

Associated Society, but entirely without consultation with the R.C.A.   Perhaps this matters the less, because neither scheme is more than a mere outline of the method of control ; but it is certainly regrettable that in the negotiations which have taken place since the end of the war, the N.U.R. and the R.C.A. should have dealt with the Government quite separately, and without any consideration or common policy.   A Railway Royal Commission, similar to the Coal Industry Commission, would be exceptionally valuable, because it would compel joint action and the preparation of a common scheme.

In dealing with railway control, then, although the issue is hardly less immediate than that of the mines, there is no satisfactory or comprehensive scheme which can be taken as a basis for discussion.   The N.U.R. plan has not even been published in full, although stray hints, references and quotations have appeared in the Press.   I shall therefore take the course of sketching, without more than incidental reference to existing schemes, the lines which an immediate scheme of railway control might reasonably follow.

In the first place, no mere scheme of central representation of the railway workers can fill the bill.   It is true that the railway service lends itself probably to a higher degree of centralisation than any other industry ; but this does not at all do away with the need for regional and local, as well as for central, control of the industry, and for the participation of the workers in control regionally and locally as well as at the centre.   The Ministry of Transport is reported to be contemplating a scheme of regional devolution.   Under such a scheme, the real detailed control, to which the railway workers would be able to make by far their most effective contribution, would to a great extent pass from the centre to the regions, and any control granted to the workers would be in practice inoperative unless it applied to the regions equally with the centre.

Moreover, if, as I assume, some of the principal gains from the participation of the workers in control will be an increased efficiency and sense of responsibility, and an increased willingness to co-operate in making the railway system a real public service, it is clearly essential that control should apply to the small unit just as much as to the large unit. The workers must be given the fullest possible control over those things which they understand best, such as the actual running of a station, a goods yard or a locomotive shed. These are, in the railway service, the equivalents of the pit in the mining industry, and no system of control which does not apply fully to them will succeed in enlisting the real co-operation of Labour in making the industry efficient.

The second condition of any effective scheme of control I have touched upon already. It is the close and friendly co-operation of the workers by hand and brain, and the sharing between them, according to their respective aptitudes and functions, of the control which may now or later be secured.

The first control demand of the railwaymen was one which was suggested, if not dictated, by war conditions. This was the demand for direct representation of the railway Trade Unions on the Railway Executive Committee—nominally a Committee of the Board of Trade, but consisting entirely of the General Managers of the principal lines. In the official declaration of policy by the N.U.R., the demand was broadened into one for equal representation, both national and local, upon the governing bodies of all railways. The need for local as well as national control was thus recognised at an early stage. The proposals put forward by the N.U.R. to the Government in the autumn of 1919, as reported in the Press, made the proposal more explicit by demanding first complete national ownership of the railways, and secondly, their control by a body of whose members half would be chosen by the railwaymen and half by the House of Commons. In none of these proposals is the position of the administrative and managerial staff directly touched upon, and upon this point we are accordingly left to make our own inferences.

The Railway Clerks' Association, as we have seen, includes not only clerks, but also a considerable proportion of the managerial and administrative grades. It does not, however, include all these grades or reach, as yet, quite to the top of the railway service. Thus, although railway Trade Unionism embraces a larger proportion than mining Trade Unionism of the elements necessary for control, it is not yet equipped for assuming complete control, and cannot be until the whole of the necessary personnel of the railways, from top to bottom, is included in it.

In discussing the mining problem, I have given my reasons for holding that the actual managing bodies in charge of the industry should not include either bureaucrats or representatives of the consumers, and that the representation of the public and of the consumers should be provided for by other methods. These arguments seem to me to have equal force in the case of the railways. The right course is to entrust the whole of the railway workers with the complete task of administration, and to put them all " upon their honour " to manage the railways as a public service. The representation of consumers and of the public can then be provided for in the way already suggested in the case of the mines, first, by national and regional Consumers' Councils representing the travelling public and the various industries principally concerned in railway transport, and secondly, by a House of Commons Committee to which the Consumers' Council could carry its complaints, and to which the ultimate financial authority, under Parliament, would belong. It is unnecessary to go into these provisions at greater length, as they have been more fully explained already in the preceding chapter.[1]

What, then, should be the composition of the Railway Executive of the future, if it is to include neither bureaucrats nor consumers, but is to consist solely of railway workers? The three railway Trade Unions and the shopmen's organisations seem to me to have a fair claim to more than half the representation on such a body. At least half the representation should go to the manual workers alone, and the supervisory and technical representatives who should form the other half of the Executive should include direct representatives of those technical and managerial grades which are organised on Trade Union lines. Only the residue, representing the top grades which are still unorganised, should be for the present nominated by the State from these grades until the complete constitution of a railway Guild becomes possible.

The regional bodies exercising control over the railway service should reproduce the same structure, except that the nominated members should, in their case, be nominated not by the State but by the central Executive. For the smaller local bodies, a greater elasticity would be required, and their composition would vary from case to case. Different representations would be required in the case

[1] See pp. 81 ff.

of, say, a station or goods yard committee on the one hand, and a railway locomotive shop committee on the other.

One of the most important elements in any scheme of railway control will be the control of promotion. As we have seen, the higher grades in the railway service are to a very great extent, and could be to an even greater extent, recruited from below. Any attempt to establish industrial democracy on the railways will have to regulate promotion on democratic lines. I do not mean by this that all supervisors and administrators will have to be chosen by a mass vote, and still less that the higher grades should be filled by co-option from above. Both these methods will probably have a part to play, varying with the functions which have to be performed by the officers whose choice is in question.

Broadly speaking, there are two types of " administrators " or " professionals," as distinguished from rank and file workers. First, there are those in whose case the factor of primary importance is technique and professional knowledge ; and, secondly, there are those whose chief function is that of organising, directing and commanding other men. The two functions are by no means mutually exclusive, and there are difficult marginal cases ; but there can be no doubt that the two types are, in general, distinct, although each usually requires in some measure at least the qualities of the other.

Thus, a foreman or a stationmaster or a manager is clearly in the first place an organiser of men. He requires technical qualifications of at least a certain order, but his main qualifications are personal rather than technical. On the other hand, a financial expert, a designer, a costings expert, and many others are in the first place technicians requiring expert knowledge, and only in the second place, if at all, commanders of men. The qualifications for their jobs are therefore in the last resort technical rather than personal.

This distinction seems to afford a basis for an approximate formula for the application of democracy to the question of promotion. This formula may be roughly stated as follows :

(1) (*a*) Where the qualifications required are primarily personal rather than technical, and where the function of the officer to be appointed is primarily that of organising other men or giving orders to " subordinates," the right principle of promotion is that of election from below.

(*b*) In so far as technical qualifications are also required for a post which falls mainly into the above class, the range of choice for the electors may legitimately be restricted to persons possessing the necessary technical qualifications ; but the choice among persons so qualified should still be made by election from below.

(2) (*a*) Where the qualifications required are primarily technical rather than personal, and where the function in question is primarily that of offering an expert opinion and not that of giving direct orders, the right general principle is that of choice by the persons possessing the technical qualifications required.

(*b*) In so far as a post falling into this second class also requires personal qualifications and is secondarily concerned with the giving of orders, the principle of professional co-option may be modified by the introduction of an element of election from below from among nominations made by the technically qualified.

I do not pretend that this formula affords more than the most general guidance. In particular, it requires further explanation on several material points. In the first place, the general principle on which it rests is that an integral part of any system of self-government is the choice of " commanders " by those over whom command is to be exercised. I do not mean by this that each " commander " must in every case be chosen by the particular group of workers over whom he is to exercise his command, although I believe that in many cases this will be found to be the best method of choice. In other cases, the electorate may be wider than the sphere in which the elected person is to have command. This applies with even greater force to the removal of a person once elected than to the initial election. I do not suggest that if a group of workers in a shop or station chooses its own foreman or stationmaster, it should also have the right to remove him without appeal or at a moment's notice. Apart from provision for periodical re-election and a regular term of office, it would be necessary to safeguard the position of any executive official by providing that he should not be dismissed during his term except after appeal and with the consent of a wider authority. Thus, a stationmaster threatened with dismissal by the rank and file workers under him should be able to appeal to the regional organisation of the railway service or to some tribunal constituted on a regional basis, and to have his case judged by that impartial tribunal. Democracy cannot do without leadership, and leadership without any security would be impossible.

Generally speaking, wherever technical qualifications are required, it should fall to the technicians themselves, through their association or institute, to lay down the qualifying tests for the holding of any position. Where

personal qualifications are required as well, the final choice
among qualified persons should be made by democratic
election. Thus, to-day a man cannot be a ship's captain
unless he holds a master's certificate ; but the fact that he
holds such a certificate is not enough to give him command
of a ship. For that a further choice is necessary. In this
case, neither is the granting of the certificate in the hands
of a body representing the masters, nor the choice of a
captain in those of the seamen. The dual principle is,
however, recognised, and these two changes would bring
it into harmony with the idea of industrial self-government.

This problem of leadership and election is not, of course,
one which affects the railways alone. It concerns every
industry and service ; and under a self-governing, or
Guild, organisation of industry it will be of vital importance
to find the best possible way of choosing those who are to
occupy official positions. No successful enterprise is ever
really managed by a Committee, and none ever will be,
whether the Committee is a board of directors or a Guild
Executive. In the last resort, the actual management will
always devolve upon the officers and administrators,
and the function of the Committee will be that of giving
them general directions as to policy and of criticising the
results which they produce. Even then a committee can
only do effectively if it is a body of persons actually con-
versant with the technique and operation of the enterprise
concerned. Beyond it they can only go in so far as, individually, the members of the Committee themselves assume
the duty of executive officers and take charge each of a
particular department of the work. Where this is the case,
the Committee as a Committee gives general directions to,
and acts as a critic of the activities of, each of its own
members as an executive officer.

I have dwelt upon this point because objection is often taken to the whole idea of industrial self-government on the ground that industry cannot be managed by committees. This is true enough ; but it is no objection to industrial self-government.   The committee is as necessary for the giving of general directions and for the criticisms of method and results as the officer with authority is necessary for getting the actual work done.   It is necessary to have both, and to ensure that both shall conform to the democratic ideal.   Such conformity does not mean that the power of the officer must be curbed ; for industrial democracy will need to trust, and to entrust wide powers to, its officers. But it does mean that the methods of choice and promotion must be democratic, that the rank and file must choose its commanders, and that the technicians must be the judges of technical qualification.

In the particular case of the railways, this question of promotion is of peculiar importance.   Recruitment for the higher posts in the railway service now takes place from four sources, two inside and two outside the service itself. The external sources are, first, the general upper-middle class, from which, largely for reasons of family and favouritism, a certain recruitment takes place ; and, secondly, certain definite professions not confined to the railways, as when a consulting engineer is brought in from outside. Self-government would do away with the first, without affecting the second, of these sources.

The internal sources are, first, the manual-working, and, secondly, the clerical grades, the bigger share in promotion going, at present, to the latter.   Clearly, it is desirable, subject to technical qualifications, that the widest possible area should be open to promotion from both these sources, and that stationmasters, for instance, should be appointed, according to their personal qualifications, from either group. A scheme of promotion, jointly planned by the Trade Unions of both manual and clerical workers, is an integral part of the control scheme upon which the railwaymen ought to be busy at the present time. Certain posts will be by their nature recruited from the manual, and certain others from the clerical grades ; but many posts, including most of those high up in the service, ought to be equally open to both groups.

It may be said that, after all the discussion in this chapter, the precise structure to be adopted in any scheme of national railway control under public ownership still remains very obscure. That is true enough so far as the details are concerned ; and I freely confess my inability to prepare a more detailed or precise scheme. No one who is not intimately acquainted with railway practice can do that. It is, indeed, essentially a task for railwaymen themselves, and these suggestions are only intended to provoke discussion and to help, I trust, towards the formulation of a scheme by those who are directly concerned. A scheme reasonably formulated jointly by the whole of the railway Trade Unions would, I believe, stand an excellent chance of adoption ; for every one recognises the present inefficiency of our transport system, and no one has much confidence in the power of either bureaucracy or private enterprise to mend it. The road therefore lies open to industrial democracy as soon as the railwaymen are ready to march along it. It is their unreadiness that holds them back.

CHAPTER VII

"ENCROACHING CONTROL" AND THE WHITLEY REPORTS

I

ENCROACHING CONTROL

THE mining and railway industries have become the chief battlegrounds of industry largely because, in both of them, the issue is comparatively simple. They are, to a far greater extent than other great industries, homogeneous and uniform ; they can be treated as wholes for the purpose of detailed, as well as of general, argument ; they can readily, if considerations of policy so dictate, be transferred to public ownership and placed under a system of democratic administration. Moreover, in both these industries there are great Trade Unions well able not only to put forward demands and to frame a policy, but to play their part in the control of the industries when they pass under public ownership. Nor is the expropriation of the present owners a difficult matter ; for their assets admit of comparatively simple valuation in accordance with general principles that can be easily laid down.

When we pass from these great public utility industries to the general run of manufacturing industries and groups, the position is far less simple. Even if an industry is itself comparatively compact and homogeneous, like the cotton industry, the commercial processes attaching to it and the marketing of its wares may be a highly complex business ; while such a group of industries as those concerned with the various forms of engineering and shipbuilding present both on their manufacturing and on their commercial sides an almost inextricable confusion. Those who advocate a drastic change in the industrial system may therefore easily be tempted to leave these industries severely alone in their arguments, and to concentrate upon those cases in which it is comparatively easy to propose an immediately practicable solution.

There are, however, two very good reasons why such an evasion cannot content us. In the first place, although a change of system may not be as immediately imminent in these cases as in those of the railways and the mines, it is bound soon to come, and it is therefore necessary to prepare for it now. Secondly, the workers in these other industries have also been fired by the idea of control, and it is therefore no less necessary to work out an immediate strategy and plan of campaign in their case than in that of the miners and the railwaymen.

In the following chapters an attempt will be made to lay down the general lines of policy suggested in the case of industries of the manufacturing type, and to apply in some measure these general suggestions to certain outstanding industries. The particular instances taken will be those already mentioned—on the one hand, the vast and complex group which passes under the name of the engineering and shipbuilding industry; and, on the other hand, the cotton industry, relatively simple in structure, but full of complexities on its commercial side. These two cases between

8

them will necessarily raise most of the major problems which arise in connection with the manufacturing industries as a whole.

It must be made clear that I do not propose to deal in the following chapters, any more than I dealt in the last, with the final or complete organisation of any industry " under Guild Socialism." My purpose in this book is that of discussing not ideals, but immediate questions of policy, and the changes which I am discussing are limited to those which are capable of being at once introduced, if only we possess the will to introduce them.

Before I begin to deal with the actual instances which I have selected, there are certain general propositions which require to be stated. It must be clear that the adoption of the measures proposed in the foregoing chapters in the cases of the mines and the railways would at once pave the way for further extensions of public ownership and democratic control. If the State did not own any industries or industrial establishments, it would be more difficult than it is to acclimatise the public mind to the idea of public ownership of mines and railways. Whatever we may think of the existing methods of Post Office and Dockyard administration, the fact that the State owns these services helps to make the public mind accessible to the idea of an extension of public ownership, particularly if the criticisms directed against bureaucratic management are satisfactorily met. Secondly, if the Trade Unions at present exercised no control over industry, it would be far more difficult than it is to get the public to accept the idea of democratic management. The fact that the public has to admit that the Trade Unions have forced their way into a certain negative control of industry, does, whether the public likes this control or not, make for the easier acceptance of the idea that this fact must be socially recognised and given its place in the new economic order.

The national ownership and more or less democratic control of mines and railways would at once carry this process several stages further, and we should almost automatically begin to regard as immediately nationalisable industries and services in connection with which the idea of national ownership at present hardly enters into our heads as an immediate possibility. I do not say that we should be led to regard *all* industries as nationalisable ; for I do not believe that *all* are nationalisable, even in the longest run. But I do hold that, until we have exhausted the list of nationalisable industries, every industry which we actually nationalise will suggest the nationalisation of another.

This, of course, is only one side of the process of mental conversion. It is equally true that every actual experiment in democratic control, whether it takes place in a nationally owned service or not, will suggest further experiments, and that the more people see democratic control actually in operation in a narrow sphere, the readier they will be to believe that it can be extended over a wider sphere. In saying this, I do not even assume its success in a high degree, as success will continue to be measured in a capitalist environment ; for actuality is a more potent influence on the average human imagination than a relative calculation of success and failure.[1]

I do not mean merely that the national ownership and democratic control of one industry or service will create

[1] Thus, the argument that a theory has never been tried, and that it is therefore impossible to know whether it would succeed or not, is often of more influence in opposition to a proposal than even the clearest demonstration that it has been tried, and is a failure.

an *economic* momentum towards the adoption of similar measures in closely related industries and services.   Doubtless, this will be the case.   Public ownership of railways will create a momentum towards public ownership of other forms of transport, both by land and by water, and perhaps towards public ownership of those industries upon which the transport services depend for their material equipment. But, in addition to the economic momentum, a *human* momentum will be created.   The demand of the workers in all other nationalisable industries and services will be stimulated, and the public imagination will be rendered more receptive of the demand.   This *human* momentum will affect not only industries closely related to those which are publicly owned and democratically controlled, but progressively all industries to which similar methods can be applied.

That is why I emphasised, in discussing the mining industry, the point that the present struggle there affects the workers in other industries, in their capacity as producers, hardly less than it affects the miners themselves. That is why all workers have rightly ranged themselves behind the miners in pressing their demand.   But, if the workers in these other industries are to reap the benefit which they can reap from the situation which exists in the mines, they must be armed with an immediate strategy of their own so devised as to pave the way for democratic control to accompany public ownership. They must not merely lay their plans for the future, but must adopt for the present a policy which will increase their power under capitalist ownership, and place in their hands a measure of control without entangling them in the present system.

This policy, applicable also with certain modifications

to industries at present controlled bureaucratically by
the State, is becoming known under the name of the
policy of *encroaching control.* In general terms, it may be
defined as a policy of transferring from the employer or
his representatives to the organised workers through their
Trade Unions and workshop organisations as many as
possible of the functions at present controlled by capitalism
in the sphere of production. This transference is, indeed,
a logical development of Trade Union activity as it has
existed in the past. The aim of the Trade Unions in the
various trades and industries has been so to organise
the workers as to control the supply of labour, and by
means of this control to prescribe conditions with which
the employer must comply in order to get labour to work
for him.   This collective control has hitherto been
exercised only within a restricted sphere—that of " collective bargaining " as it has hitherto been understood. The
Trade Unions have prescribed minimum rates of wages,
maximum hours of labour, definite conditions governing
overtime, apprenticeship, the class of workers to be
employed on a particular operation, and so forth ; but,
having laid down these general minimum standards, they
have, apart from occasional intervention arising out of actual
disputes, left the management of industry in the employer's
hands, allowed him to engage and dismiss workers individually as he has thought fit, accepted his claim to control
promotion and to appoint supervisors and managers—
to say nothing of his claim, when the wages due have been
paid, to have sole control of the product resulting from
the application of *their* labour to " *his* " plant.

As soon as the workers take up the standpoint of encroaching control, the question at once arises how far
they can or should take out of the employers' hands and

transfer to themselves collectively, wholly or in part, any of the functions mentioned above, or others like them. In discussing any such question, there are four principal considerations which naturally present themselves to the workers. First, have they the power to take over a particular function ? Secondly, have they the skill and ability to perform the function when they have taken it over ? Thirdly, what will be the effect of their assumption of it upon their status and economic power ? And fourthly, what will be the wider social effects in relation to their ideal of the economic system which they desire to bring into existence ? The latter two considerations especially involve a full understanding of any danger that a particular assumption of control may result, not in a weakening of capitalist control, but in a strengthening of it by the cementing of an alliance between capitalists and workers at the public expense.

This exposition may appear, at the present stage, somewhat academic ; but it will be easier to make plain its practical application in dealing with particular industries and problems. What I want to make plain at present is the sharp distinction which exists between this policy of *encroaching control* and the policy underlying the Whitley Report, with which persistent attempts are made to confuse it. It is necessary to clear this misconception out of the way before we can proceed to our constructive discussions.

II

The Whitley Reports

Readers whose knowledge of the industrial situation in Great Britain is confined to the speeches of Cabinet

Ministers and the comments of the daily Press are even
now apt to imagine that a new Heaven and a new earth
are being created by some magical process initiated by
the Whitley Report. Joint Standing Industrial Councils
representing employers and employed, so the Press and
the politicians inform us, are being set up almost every
day, and a new spirit of fellowship and goodwill is
animating masters and workmen alike. I can only say
that I have sought for this new spirit, and I have not
found it. Joint Standing Industrial Councils are indeed
being established in considerable numbers ; but most of
the vital industries have hitherto shown no anxiety to
establish them, and, even where they have been established,
there is not much evidence of the "new spirit" of which
we hear so much.

In fact, the Whitley Report, loudly as it has been
acclaimed in governmental circles, has almost entirely
failed to stir the world of Labour. In some industries,
notably in the mining and railway industries and in the
big engineering and metal-working group, it has been
definitely rejected. In other cases it has been accepted
as a harmless piece of machinery, but without any particular
enthusiasm, and certainly with no idea that it provides a
panacea for all industrial troubles. The only case in
which its adoption has been urgently pressed for by the
workers is that of State employees, and in this instance
the urgency arises largely from the desire to use it as a
means of securing full recognition and the right of collective
bargaining, and from the fact that there is in such cases
no system of private profit-making in which the workers
can run the risk of becoming entangled.

The first Whitley Report, to which the later reports
were hardly more than supplements, proposed that, in

the better organised industries, Standing Joint Industrial Councils should be set up nationally in each industry, with District Councils and Works Councils under them. The National and District Councils were to consist of an equal representation from Employers' Associations on the one side and from Trade Unions on the other. They were to be voluntary in character, and the endowing of their decisions with any legal power was to be a matter for further consideration. The State was not to be represented, and was to appoint a chairman only when requested to do so by the Council itself. At the same time, the Government announced its intention of recognising the Councils as advisory bodies representing the various industries, and of consulting them on matters affecting their interests.

In all this there was nothing in the smallest degree startling or novel. In most industries in Great Britain there have long existed regular means of joint negotiation and consultation between employers and employed. In some cases these have taken the form of Boards of Conciliation with agreed rules and methods of procedure : in others, there have been merely regular arrangements for periodic conference. The important point is that, in the majority of organised industries, recognition of Trade Unionism and frequent negotiation between Trade Unions and Employers' Associations have long been the rule.

The Whitley Report did not in reality carry matters any further than most industries had gone already, though at first sight it may have seemed to do so. It hinted again and again that one of its principal reasons for urging the establishment of Joint Industrial Councils was in order to satisfy the demand of the workers for a greater control over industry ; but it was not proposed to transfer

to the workers any definite powers, and the actual constitutions of the Whitley Councils which have been
established do nothing at all to make this aspiration a
fact. They provide indeed for joint consideration of
questions affecting the industry ; but they do nothing
to affect the final and exclusive control of the employer
over the way in which he runs his business.

I am not complaining, or saying that they could do
more. I am merely criticising the prevalent view that the
Whitley Report makes a new and revolutionary departure
in the sphere of industrial relations. It does not : it only
regularises and formalises a process which has long been
going on in most of our principal industries, and one which
would have continued whether there had been a Whitley
Report or not.

In fact, the control of industry cannot be altered merely
by the setting up of joint committees. The control of
industry rests on the economic power of those who control
it ; and only a shifting of the balance of economic power
will alter this control. Such a shifting of power may be,
and I believe is, in progress at the present time ; but it is
quite independent of such events as the issuing and adoption by the Government of the Whitley Report. The
view most current among Trade Unionists — that the
Whitley Report does not matter much one way or the
other—is certainly the right one.

Nevertheless, though it is not likely to produce large
permanent results, the Report has, for the time being,
attracted a good deal of attention. Official Trade Unionism, represented by the Parliamentary Committee of the
Trades Union Congress, accepted it without enthusiasm
and subject to its remaining purely voluntary. Even the
mildest of Trade Union leaders refuse to tolerate compulsory

arbitration in any form, except under protest as a war measure. Unofficial " rank and file " Trade Unionism, represented by the Shop Stewards' movement and other agencies, roundly denounced " Whitleyism " as an attempt to side-track the growing movement of the class-conscious workers towards the control of industry. " Whitleying away our strength," one rank and file critic entitled his article upon the Report, and went on to urge that the capitalists, fearing the rising tide of rank and file committees, had inspired the Report in the hope of substituting for them joint committees of masters and men, and so depriving them of their dynamic and revolutionary character. The National Guilds League, also representing the left wing, declared against the underlying assumption of the Report that industrial peace is possible and desirable under capitalism, and pointed out that, whatever the merits or demerits of joint committees, they cannot provide the dynamic for securing control, or offer any alternative to workshop agitation and workshop organisation for the purpose of a gradual assumption of control by the workers. Other critics, largely among State Socialists, dwelt rather on the dangers of Whitleyism to the consumer, and the risk of establishing a common solidarity between employers and workers in a particular industry against the public— in a demand for a tariff, for instance, or in a conspiracy to keep prices high—a risk also noted by the Guild Socialists, but regarded by them as small owing to the hostility of Labour to such anti-social projects. In fact, everywhere the left wing, and often a part of the right also, rejected the assumptions of the Whitley Report.

What, then, of the Whitley Councils and other bodies on similar lines which have been established ? The first thing to notice about them is that most of them affect only small and often ill-organised groups. The Whitley Committee itself recommended the establishment of Joint Industrial Councils only in those industries in which employers and employed were comparatively well organised. For the industries in which organisation was weak, it recommended the establishment of Trade Boards. Nevertheless, Whitley Councils have been established in a number of industries which cannot by any means be regarded as well organised. Instances of this are the Pottery Council and the Match Makers' Council. Moreover, Councils are being set up for certain small sectional trades which can hardly by any stretch of imagination be regarded as industries. The Bobbin Industrial Council and the Spelter Industrial Council are notable examples of this undue tendency to sectional organisation. On the other hand, councils have been set up in a few important groups, including the woollen, printing, baking and other industries. The Building Council, which is not really a Whitley Council at all, stands in a class by itself, and is dealt with separately later in this book.

In addition to the Industrial Councils set up under the Whitley scheme, the Government, through the Ministry of Reconstruction, established a number of " Interim Reconstruction Committees," principally in industries in which the formation of Industrial Councils was not found possible, but also in some cases for small or almost unorganised industrial groups, such as " Needles and Fishhooks " and " Furniture Removing and Warehousing." The number of these committees, which were brought into existence as temporary bodies, grows steadily less as they either dissolve or form themselves into full Industrial Councils, of which there are now about fifty in existence.

It is already possible to pass a fairly conclusive judgment upon the Industrial Councils and their possibilities. Their constitutions were, as a rule, drawn so as to embrace a large variety of purposes, without giving much indication of the course which they would actually pursue. One significant clause, which occurs in the constitution of several Councils, makes it one of the objects to maintain selling prices at a level which will secure reasonable remuneration to both employers and employees. This recalls the professed objects of many trusts and employers' combinations too closely to require detailed criticism ; but it is important to note it because it is clearly based on the assumption of a common interest between employers and workers in a particular industry—a common interest which clearly might easily become anti-social in its effects, and in any case runs counter to the Socialist theory of a common solidarity of all workers irrespective of craft or industry. Apart from this provision, the constitutions contain few notable features, except that in many cases the provisions for District Councils and, still more, the provisions for Work Committees are allowed to fall very much into the background. Indeed, although the Whitley scheme made it perfectly clear that Works and District Councils were regarded as being fully as important as National Councils, few of the existing Whitley Councils have as yet brought district or works bodies into effective existence.

Moreover, the activities of Whitley Councils up to the present time—with the single exception of the Building Council or Parliament, which was, in origin, not a Whitley Council at all—do not indicate the likelihood of any important practical results. It has already been found on more than one occasion that, as soon as a real industrial issue is raised

by either side, a deadlock is quite as likely to ensue on an
Industrial Council as it was formerly in a Conciliation Board
of Joint Conference.   Already, Councils have come to ship-
wreck owing to disagreements beteeen the two sides ;
and, where they have remained in being, they have been
suspended while other means were found of settling the
difference or of fighting it out.

It is, in fact, becoming more and more evident that
Whitley Councils are not really bodies of any considerable
importance, and that the large promises which were made
at the time of their inception had no substance behind them.
In some quarters, it is suggested that the remedy lies in
giving to their decisions a mandatory power and making
them enforceable upon the whole of the industries which
they represent ; but there are few who seriously regard this
course as practicable.   The general opinion in the Labour
world is that the Whitley Report can be safely ignored.   It
has added a few fresh joint bodies to the large number
which previously existed in the various industries ; but in
their actual working most of the new industrial Councils
hardly differ in any vital particular from the old Conciliation
Boards and Conferences for which they were supposed to
provide a vastly superior substitute.

The moral of this failure is obvious.   There is no way out
of the industrial deadlock by the creation of joint bodies of
private employers and Trade Unions.   The divergence of
interests and points of view between the two parties effectively prevents real co-operation, and attempts at joint
action break down as soon as they are confronted with any
real problem.

In fact, all these movements for " industrial harmony "
are of little or no effect in relation to the really vital
problems of industry.   Whatever joint machinery may

be set up, it will hardly affect the real relations of the parties which now confront each other in the industrial world.

Employers and workers will continue to differ about their relative status in industry and about their respective shares of its fruits ; and they will continue to settle their differences mainly by the balancing of economic forces, whether the balancing is done by negotiation or by the open force of strike or lock-out.   In fact, those who attach much importance to joint machinery such as that which was recommended in the Whitley Reports, are apt to forget that no amount of machinery can alter the essential facts of the economic situation.

III

THE FALLACY OF JOINT CONTROL

In its prompt repudiation of the principles upon which the Whitley Report was explicitly based, the National Guilds League stated, as clearly as it is possible to state, the fundamental divergence of view between the Government idea of Reconstruction and the idea which animates all that is best in the Labour Movement.   It concentrated attention upon the fundamental fact (not a mere theory) of the class struggle in industry, and it expressly repudiated the idea of any possible " permanent improvement " in the relationships between employers and Trade Unionists.

But it did not stop there.   It realised that Trade Unionists would be confronted with the necessity for defining their policy in relation to actual schemes based more or less closely upon the proposals of the Whitley Report.   The clear statement of principle which is enunciated in the

" Observations "[1] would not by itself have provided Trade Unionists who found themselves in such a position with the ammunition required for riddling actual schemes based upon it.

The " Notes for Trade Unionists " were issued to supply this need. They reasserted in a shorter form the principle which had been fully expounded in the " Observations "; but in addition they formulated an actual policy which it would be possible for Trade Unionists to follow out, in meeting suggestions for the establishment of Joint Industrial Councils in their own particular trades. Briefly stated, the view enunciated in the second pamphlet was that no form of joint machinery could in any way satisfy the working-class demand for control of industry, which could only be met by an actual transference of powers from the employers to the workers, in such a way that the workers would enter upon an encroaching control of functions hitherto exercised by the capitalists or their nominees.

It thus clearly dissociated the proposals for joint machinery from the question of control, whereas the whole effect of the Whitley Report had been to confuse the two things, and make it seem that the working-class aspiration for control could be satisfied by the setting up of joint machinery. When once the clear separation of the two things is realised, when it is understood that joint machinery, whatever its character, has nothing to do with the working-class demand for control, and can therefore afford no possible substitute for it, the way is clear for the consideration of joint machinery on its merits, and apart from

[1] The references here are to two useful pamphlets on the Whitley Report issued by the National Guilds League, and now published in a single booklet under the title *National Guilds or Whitley Councils.*

the presuppositions and prejudices which are imported by a confusion between it and control.

The main point made in the " Notes for Trade Unionists " in dealing with this question, was that the Trade Unionist's first duty is to set his own house in order, and to get his industrial organisation based on such principles as will remove the danger that is inherent in joint machinery where Trade Unionism is not organised on an inclusive industrial basis. The safeguards and restrictions which were laid down in the " Notes for Trade Unionists " were sufficient to ensure that any joint machinery set up in accordance with them, so far from helping Capitalism to rivet the chains upon Labour, would have merely the effect of improving the methods of negotiation without imposing any disabilities upon the workers. Whether joint machinery, even of this character, is desirable is not a question that could be answered either with a plain affirmative or with a plain negative. The answer depends upon the particular circumstances of each case. Even the most advanced Trade Unionists accept the necessity for some form of joint machinery in certain cases : they may object strongly, as Guildsmen do, to existing methods of conciliation, they may desire to sweep away Boards of Conciliation, which have the effect of tieing the workers' hands, but since they demand recognition of Trade Unions and of shop stewards, they must inevitably contemplate joint machinery with the employers, and the possibility of some joint machinery for the purpose of such negotiation.

The main point is to get clearly in mind the fact that joint machinery is purely an instrument for negotiating with the employer, and is in no sense a way by which the workers can enter upon the control of industry. The attempts of the Press and of the Government advocates to confuse the minds of Trade Unionists by pretending that the Whitley scheme provides for control by Trade Unionists were the merest camouflage ; and those who took up this attitude were merely trying to divert the workers' endeavours into comparatively harmless channels.

Whitley Report or no Whitley Report, the main thing for the working-class is still the improvement of its own industrial organisation, and the building up of a movement which is at once organised on the right lines, and equipped with the right strategy. Such organisation alone can make for any " Reconstruction " that is worthy of the name. The working-class movement cannot, any more than any other movement, make bricks without straw. It will take hard thought and hard work, and constant endeavour by those Trade Unionists who realise the fundamental purpose of their Unions, to build up the sort of industrial organisation which will be able to secure an effective voice in the control of industry.

The Whitley Reports may, in the long run, prove to have helped in this task, not because the organisations based upon them will be of any use, but because they will have served to clarify the issues, and because the exposure of the suggestions for joint control which are being founded on them will bring more clearly than ever to the front the nature of the working-class demand for encroaching control. Those workers who get Whitley Councils and those who do not get them will learn that joint action with their employers cannot bring them any real change in status. It may improve and make more smooth the machinery of negotiation, but it will not alter any of the fundamental factors of the wage relation. Seeing this, the workers will turn with renewed vigour to the development of their own

9

Trade Union machinery, and will take in hand energetically the framing of a policy directed to the securing of an encroaching control over industry.

The thing we have fundamentally to bother about is the lessening of the authority and the functions of Capitalism, and the increasing of the functions and the economic power of the working-class. Concentration upon this does not absolve us from the necessity of watching very carefully the schemes which are put forward in the name of the employers or of the Government, and of taking up an attitude to these schemes in the light of the immediate necessities of the case ; but we must not allow our preoccupation with such immediate schemes to divert our main attention from our fundamental object—the abolition of the wage system—or from the constructive steps which the working-class itself must take with a view to securing that object.

CHAPTER VIII

ENGINEERING AND SHIPBUILDING

I

THE INDUSTRIES AND THEIR ORGANISATION

THE preceding chapter was, to a great extent, devoted to clearing the ground. We are now, with the Whitley Reports put safely out of the way, in a position to discuss directly the position which exists in such an industry as engineering—which, indeed, is not really an industry at all, but a great group of industries and trades running one into another and overlapping with many other industries. It will be best to begin with a brief survey of the complexities of the industry itself.

Outside engineering, as we are dealing with it here, fall those forms of metal working which are concerned not with the making of manufactured metal goods, but with the making of iron and steel, and of certain iron and steel products, directly or indirectly from the ore. We are thus not concerned with blast-furnaces, smelting-works, rolling-mills, tube-works, tinplate-works, and the rest of the factories which are generally regarded as belonging to the iron and steel industry. It is difficult to draw a line; but these at least have to a certain extent a common character of their own which clearly mark them off from

engineering.   We are, on the other hand, closely concerned
with all those factories which are employed in the making of machines—machine-tools, hydraulic plant, agricultural machinery, textile machinery, electrical machinery,
sewing-machines, motor vehicles, aircraft, and a host of
others.   In this sphere, the manufacture of railway locomotives and other appliances forms a disputed territory
between the engineering and railway industries.   Iron-
founding, though it may be regarded as forming to some
extent a separate group, is so closely interwoven with
general engineering, and presents such similar problems
from the Trade Union point of view, that it may conveniently be treated as falling within the scope of this
chapter.   Through the light - castings trades — baths,
stoves, grates, etc.—this establishes a close relation between
the engineering and building industries.

What is said in this chapter also applies generally to
brassworks and to a considerable extent to the vast mis-
cellaneous group of the minor metal trades—sheet-metal
working in its various forms, and the small Black Country
industries in general.   Again, vehicle building is every
year becoming more closely allied to engineering as metal
plays in it a more and more important part.

Distinct from engineering, but very closely allied to it
through marine engineering, is the shipbuilding industry,
including both the private shipbuilding firms and the
Royal Dockyards.   This, again, has very similar labour
problems to engineering, with which it is, on the Trade
Union and on the employers' side alike, inseparably bound
up by overlapping organisation.   It also therefore falls
within the scope of this chapter.

On the employers' side, the organisation of this great
group of industries is simple, so far as its dealings with

Labour are concerned. There are, indeed, very large numbers of special associations dealing with particular groups and products, or with particular markets, for trading and price-fixing purposes; but for negotiation there are only two organisations of really considerable importance. These are, first, the Engineering and National Employers' Federation, formed during the war by the amalgamation of two bodies organising respectively engineering in the narrower sense and the minor metal trades; and, secondly, the Shipbuilding Employers' Federation. Neither includes all the firms in the groups with which it deals; but both are very powerful and representative bodies.

On the Trade Union side, organisation is still chaotic. There are well over a hundred Trade Unions primarily concerned with organising workers in the engineering and shipbuilding group, and many additional Unions have members in the group. Moreover, the great majority of the less skilled workers are organised not in these Unions, but in the big general labour Unions which cut across nearly all industrial divisions.

By far the largest single Union belonging to the group is the Amalgamated Society of Engineers, which has 320,000 members, mostly skilled workers. This Society is now carrying through an amalgamation with a number of smaller Societies, and the new Union which will result will have at least 400,000 members. This, however, will still leave a large number of Societies outside, even in the engineering group in the narrower sense.

Next in size is the principal Society in the shipyard group, the United Society of Boilermakers, with almost 100,000 members. This Society is now negotiating an amalgamation with the two next largest Societies in the shipyard group, and a new Society of 150,000 members may result.

In the foundry group, the Friendly Society of Iron-founders has about 35,000 members, and there is a Federation of Foundry Trade Unions representing the group as a whole. In this case, again, amalgamation is being discussed.

Apart from these and many other metal-workers' Societies, the various wood-working and other building Unions have large numbers of members, especially in the shipyards, among joiners, painters, plumbers, furnishing trades, etc. Moreover, as we have seen, the great mass of the less skilled workers is organised in such Unions as the General Workers' Union, Workers' Union, National Amalgamated Union of Labour or National Federation of Women Workers. With the exception of the last-named, these now generally act together through the National Federation of General Workers.

There does exist one Federation—the Federation of Engineering and Shipbuilding Trades—which attempts to represent the whole, or almost the whole, of this motley assembly. This Federation includes most of the important Societies mentioned above, except the Amalgamated Society of Engineers and some of the general labour Unions. It does not, however, although it acts as a co-ordinating agency, as a rule negotiate directly with the employers, most negotiations being conducted by particular groups of Trade Unions which meet the employers under an agreement. The Shipyard Agreement and the Central Conference agreement for engineering are the principal instances of this procedure.

It will be seen that, in face of this chaotic organisation on the Trade Union side, it is very difficult for any constructive policy to be adopted by Labour. With the skilled crafts divided one from another, and with a much wider gulf between the skilled and the less skilled workers, the task of propounding any constructive policy directed to the securing of control looks almost insuperable. The carrying through of the projected amalgamations will very greatly improve the position so far as the skilled workers are concerned ; but by itself it will do nothing to bring skilled and less skilled together.

Nevertheless, the demand for control is certainly more vigorous in the engineering and shipbuilding group than anywhere else outside the mines, the railways and the Post Office. It has arisen spontaneously in the workshops, with little or no encouragement from the leaders, and often with little or no conception of the line of policy to be pursued. Before we can begin to suggest a constructive programme, we must examine the manner in which this demand has arisen, and the forms of organisation through which it is finding expression.

II

THE SHOP STEWARDS' MOVEMENT

The outstanding development of organisation in the engineering group during the war period is the Shop Stewards' movement. This movement, while it is not wholly new, has during the last few years assumed new forms which have very largely changed its character. For many years before the war it was the practice for certain Trade Unions and in certain districts to appoint, in addition to the ordinary Trade Union officials, workshop stewards, or delegates, in the various factories. The principal duty of these stewards was to see that newcomers joined the Union and that members paid their contributions promptly. In most cases they had no power of negotiation on behalf of the Union, though in a few trades their functions were wider, and an able man could raise the post of steward to a certain degree of importance. On the whole, it may be said that before the war, while the shop steward existed as an institution, he had shown few signs of the importance which he has acquired during the war period.

Abnormal conditions have, no doubt, had much to do with the rapid growth of the Shop Stewards' movement during the war. The rapid changes in workshop organisation, due to changes in productive methods and to the growth of dilution, the restrictive conditions imposed by the Munitions of War Acts and other war-time enactments, and the general intensification of industrial life, all gave rise to a large number of workshop problems calling for immediate action and solution. Moreover, war-time conditions to some extent hampered the freedom of the official Trade Union movement and, by increasing its remoteness from workshop life, forced the rank and file workers to the improvisation of a substitute. Thus, while the creation of official shop stewards under the old rules went on apace, there also sprang into prominence a new type of steward, unofficial or at the most semi-official, arrogating to himself considerably wider powers ; and the growth of this type of stewards naturally operated to cause an extension in the powers of stewards of the old official type.

Thus there grew up, in most important factories, a body of shop stewards only imperfectly co-ordinated with the Trade Union movement outside the workshops. Nor did the new movement stop short at this point. The "rank and file " stewards from the various factories in a district came together during the war to form a local " Shop Stewards and Workers' Committee," which in some cases became a powerful rival to the official District Committees of the various Trade Unions. And, finally, repeated and more or less successful attempts have been made to link up the various Workers' Committees in a single national " rank and file " organisation, independent in its action of the national Trade Unions to which its members continue to belong.

The policy of the Shop Stewards and Workers' Committee movement has been throughout aggressive and militant. It is a " rank and file " organisation, in revolt against the slowness and sectionalism of official Trade Unionism. In particular, its members stand for amalgamation of Trade Union forces, and for the supersession of a narrow Craft Unionism by broader forms of organisation by industry or class. One of the greatest obstacles to efficient Trade Union action during the war lay in the multiplicity of competing and often hostile Trade Unions, and the difficulty of securing a common policy among these Unions was one of the principal factors in forcing the Shop Stewards' movement on to unofficial lines. Officialism has too often meant also sectionalism and lack of co-ordination ; and, consequently, movements based on a wider idea than that of craft have been almost forced to be unofficial, at least in their early stages.

Such is the Shop Stewards' movement which the war has created. It remains to see what permanent form it will assume and what will be its permanent place in Trade Union organisation. Already it has received a considerable measure of official Trade Union recognition. The principal engineering Trade Unions have signed an un-

satisfactory agreement with the Engineering Employers
Federation providing for the recognition of shop stewards
and Works Committees in workshop negotiations. With
this recognition of shop stewards by the employers necessarily goes the recognition of shop stewards and Works
Committees by the Trade Unions themselves, as an
essential part of Trade Union official machinery.

The Shop Stewards' movement has rightly become connected in the public mind with the advocacy of militant
industrial action and with a subversive economic philosophy. This does not mean that every shop steward is
animated by revolutionary ideas, but that the general
direction of the movement has been hitherto advanced
and the temper of its leaders, who are in many cases adherents of the Socialist Labour Party, revolutionary. The
creation of shop stewards indeed resulted from a spontaneous workshop impulse in the majority of cases, and
shop stewards, both official and unofficial, are of all sorts
and of all economic philosophies—or of none. But, so
far as the central Shop Stewards' movement is concerned
a definite point of view has been developed.

First on the Clyde, but subsequently in many of the
important centres, there have grown up unofficial Workers
Committees, consisting of stewards from the various works
in a district. These Workers' Committees have taken the
lead in the " rank and file " movements during the war
period and have linked up into a provisional national organisation. The philosophy of this movement, as expressed
in the pamphlet on *The Workers' Committee*, written by
Mr. J. T. Murphy, of Sheffield, one of the principal leaders
of the shop stewards, is that all final authority should be
vested in the workers in the shops, that Trade Union
organisation should have throughout a workshop basis,

and that the instruments of advanced action should be Workers' Committees, consisting of delegates from the shops, and representing all grades of workers, skilled or unskilled, men or women.

This attitude has arisen partly because of the short-comings of Trade Union organisation, and partly because of the special conditions created by the war. In the first place, the craft basis of Trade Unionism in the metal industries has meant that authority has been divided between a huge number of separate and sometimes un-friendly Unions, while the separate organisation of skilled and unskilled is contrary to the " Industrial Unionist " theories which dominate the younger men. Secondly, the official Trade Unions were seriously hampered by war-time restrictions, and this facilitated the growth of an unofficial, " guerilla " organisation, not hampered by, and not amenable to, war-time discipline.

But, even if the growth of workshop organisation was largely the product of war conditions, there can be no doubt at all that it has come to stay. Indeed, this is generally recognised on all sides. The Trade Unions realise that in future much greater power will have to be exercised by the shop steward and the Works Committee, while the employers see that they are compelled to recognise Trade Union shop stewards as entitled to negotiate on behalf of the workers in the shop or works.

Among the adherents of the workshop movement, there is considerable divergence of opinion on the question of recognition, whether by the Trade Unions or the employer. Many of the shop stewards hold that it is better, for the present at least, that their organisations should remain unofficial, lest they be sterilised and subordinated to the control of official Trade Unionism. The advanced stewards look forward to the reorganisation of Trade Unionism on a class basis, with the seat of authority retained in the workshops, and they hold that until the craft Unions are transformed in both structure and idea the workshop movement should remain unofficial, as a sort of " ginger " element. On the other side, it is urged that if the stewards are fully recognised in their Unions, they are strong enough to force the pace from inside, and to transform the Union organisation in the way which they desire. It now seems almost certain that official shop stewards and Works Committees will be the predominant type, but that unofficial Workers' Committees co-ordinating the various shops and unofficial stewards in certain cases will for some time continue in existence.

The shop stewards, then, are certainly destined to play an important part in the engineering movement in the future. What, we must ask, is their real significance ? It lies in their position as representatives directly chosen by the Trade Unionists in the various workshops and factories. The whole orientation of the new forces in the Trade Union world is towards the securing by Labour of a greater measure of control over the actual conduct of industry. As soon as this demand for control begins to translate itself from theory into practice it must assume a " workshop " form. The only place in which Trade Unionists in " factory " industries can effectively begin to exercise control is in the workshops.

The real significance, therefore, of the Shop Stewards' movement lies in the fact that it does provide at least the nucleus of the machinery through which Trade Unionists can hope, by gradual extensions of their power, to assume control in the workshops. It may be agreed that it is at present ill-prepared for any such drastic step, and that the chaos of Trade Union organisation in the industries concerned puts huge difficulties in the way ; but, wherever the movement shows real signs of stability, the more far-seeing stewards are beginning to work out the immediate problems of control. This is the case especially where systems of payment by results are in operation ; for the demand is being made by the more constructive stewards that the working of such systems shall pass, by way of collective bargaining, into the hands of workshop committees consisting of stewards directly representing the workers employed in the shops. Another proposal of immediate workshop importance is that the appointment of charge-hands and workshop foremen shall be transferred from the management to the workers employed in the shops, that is, virtually, that the shop stewards shall take the place of the foremen appointed by the management.

Whatever the immediate fate of these proposals may be, there can be no doubt that the effect of the shop stewards' emergence will be seen in a far greater concentration of Trade Union activity on problems of workshop control, and a consequently greater orientation of the engineering Trade Union movement in the direction of control. The only things that can prevent a considerable increase in Trade Union control over industry are bad organisation and dissension in the ranks of the workers. The chances that these will be avoided we shall be better able to estimate when we have discussed the second new movement of the war period—the growth of organisation and consciousness among the less skilled workers— and its effects upon relations between the less skilled workers and skilled craftsmen who form the greater part of the Shop Stewards' movement.

III

THE RISE OF THE " LESS SKILLED "

There are many reasons which make the organisation of
skilled workers far easier than that of the less skilled.   The
skilled workmen are better paid, and can therefore more
easily afford to pay a regular contribution.   Moreover,
they often pay a high contribution, receiving in return not
only dispute benefit, but also insurance against unemployment, sickness and old age ; and, whatever the disadvantages of the mingling of " friendly " and fighting
activities may be, it undoubtedly conduces to stability and
permanence of organisation, as well as to conservatism of
spirit.   Yet again, the skilled workers have a closer bond
of craft pride and craft interest than is possible for the less
skilled workers.

This, of course, is commonplace.   What needs explaining
is not the fact that organisation has usually been weak
among the less skilled workers, but the fact that during the
years preceding the war, and still more during the war period,
it has made remarkable strides.   The number of members
in the " general labour " Unions, which represent principally
this type of workers, rose from 118,000 in 1910 to
366,000 in 1914, and the total is now considerably more
than a million and a quarter.   Why has this extraordinary
growth taken place ?

The principal explanation of the pre-war growth lies in
the increasing prevalence of industrial unrest during the
years preceding the war.   Industrial unrest, which some
call " the swing of the pendulum " of public opinion from
political to industrial action, always means, naturally, a
large accession to Trade Union membership.   To this must

be added as a further cause the fact that the sharp line of cleavage between the skilled and the unskilled was gradually being blurred, and that the tendency of machinery and management was towards the creation of a growing body of semi-skilled workers, recruited from the ranks of the unskilled, who encroached on the trades of the skilled workers, and at the same time very greatly reduced the proportion of really unskilled workers in industry. Together with the growth of " semi-skill " went a tendency towards organisation, not so strong as that of the skilled workers, but still appreciable and definite.

The creation of " semi-skill " was, of course, a process enormously accelerated by the war. Practically all the pre-war workers in the war industries were absorbed into jobs which were at least semi-skilled, and the lower ranges of jobs were more and more filled either by newcomers to industry, whether girls or adults, or by workers transferred from inessential or " sweated " trades. The whole body of semi-skilled and unskilled workers gained greatly in status as a result of war conditions. Also their pay in most cases increased ; and, even where this increase was offset by the rise in the cost of living, the expenditure of a few pence weekly on Trade Union membership seemed a far smaller thing than before.

At the same time, a common consciousness began to grow up among the less skilled workers. They found the attitude of the old-established Unions towards them often hard and unsympathetic, because the skilled men often felt that the less skilled were doing them out of their jobs, and feared the cutting of rates by their competition in the crafts. The general labour Unions therefore grew, as it were, facing both ways. They confronted the employers with demands for better conditions ; but they also con-

fronted the skilled Unions with claims for better consideration. Their consciousness of their common opportunity
and their common danger in industry took the place of
craft spirit, and acted as a powerful incentive to combination.

What relation, then, does this mass of newly organised
workers, a considerable proportion of which is concentrated in the engineering industry, bear, and what relation
is it likely to bear, to the older established Trade Unions
and to the rank and file movements discussed in the preceding section? Clearly, there are large possible divergences of attitude between them, and these divergences,
without wise handling, may easily become divergences of
actual policy.

The official Trade Unionism of the skilled workers is
apt to ignore, if not to repudiate, the claims of the less
skilled. Its members suspended during the war many of
their customs and regulations, which it had cost them
more than half a century of struggle to establish. They
received in return the right to insist that these customs and
regulations should be restored intact at the end of the war.
To this they were clearly entitled; but their reasoning
is apt to stop at that point, and to pay too little regard
to the practical expediencies and exigences of the situation.

The less skilled workers, on the other hand, conscious
both of pre-war repression and of war-time service, are apt
to take up the standpoint of holding their gains. "*J'y suis
j'y reste,*" some of them say in effect to the skilled workers.
" We could not trust our interests in your hands before the
war, and we cannot trust them now. The war has brought
us into a position from which you selfishly excluded us before
the war, and we are not prepared, because pledges have
been given which do not bind us, to revert to our pre-

war conditions of servitude and inferiority." The case
is not always so plainly stated; but that is the case,
reduced to its essential elements.

Clearly, this is a position which presents considerable
dangers to the Trade Union movement. While the skilled
and the less skilled workers spend time and effort in inter-
necine struggles, the employers will reconstruct industry
according to their own plans, and Labour will have no
effective voice in its reconstruction. Indeed, the absence
of any concerted plan of campaign in the engineering
industry to-day is largely traceable to this lack of coherence.

This point, however, must not be pressed too far. It
is still possible, and even likely, that the official Trade
Unionism of the skilled workers and the official Trade
Unionism of the less skilled, realising their common danger,
will reach at least a temporary agreement, and meet the
employers with a common programme, in which each will
concede something to the other. This is strongly to be
hoped; and for this the best elements in both sections are
working. But, even if a temporary agreement is reached,
and skilled and less skilled co-operate effectively in dealing
with their common problems, there will still remain big
differences between them which it is essential to transcend
if the recurrence of trouble is to be avoided.

The plain fact is that while the Trade Unionism of the
skilled workers is built upon a basis of craft which excludes
and antagonises the unskilled, the Trade Unionism of
the less skilled workers has hitherto been partly based
upon this antagonism. Leaders in the general workers'
Unions have often dwelt upon the function of the general
labour Union in protecting the less skilled workers, not
only against the employer, but against the skilled workers.
The two forms of organisation have thus hitherto been

10

built upon ideas which are mutually exclusive and partly antagonistic.

This means that in neither is there any permanent resting place.   The idea of craft and the idea of " no-craft " are alike inadequate to fit modern industrial conditions, or to fuse into a common programme of a lasting kind. The need is for a bigger idea, and for a bigger basis of combination, to replace both alike.

We saw, in the last section, how the "rank and file " movement which has its origin and its main strength among the skilled workers is largely based on the repudiation of the " craft " principle and on the assertion of the rival principles of class and industry.   We saw also that a considerable "rank and file " movement exists among the less skilled workers, though it is not yet so strongly organised as are the shop stewards of the skilled trades. The main difference is that, whereas the younger skilled workers tend to favour the expansion of their own Unions from a craft to an industrial basis within the industry, so as to include all the workers in the industry, whatever their degree of skill, the unskilled are led by their present form of association, which extends over most industries, to look forward rather to the combination in " One Big Union " of all workers, without regard to skill or industry. Reconciliation of these two problems is by no means impossible ; but the difference of attitude is at present a barrier to effective common action and to the unity of all the advanced forces.

Union by class—the " One Big Union " idea—involves too sharp a break with the present to be immediately practicable.   Union by industry can hardly be accomplished, in some industries at least, in face of the present strength of the general labour Unions.   The moral seems to be that the process of consolidation must be pushed as far as possible in each camp separately on the official side, and that in the Shop Stewards' and Workshop Committee movement the two must find their immediate field for common action and for propaganda. In the end, I believe that the " One Big Union " idea, for the greater part of industry at all events, will prove to be the only way of straightening out the tangle of Trade Union organisation; but the time for that is not yet, and can only come after a great central consolidation of the forces of Labour.

It may be a matter for surprise that I have said nothing about the women workers as a distinct factor. The truth is that only in one respect can they be regarded as a distinct factor; generally speaking, the women in the war trades count mainly as a section of the less skilled workers, a majority of those who are organised being found in the general labour Unions which admit both sexes, and only a minority, though an active one, in the National Federation of Women Workers. The respect in which the position of some women is different from that of the less skilled men, is that, as the men have passed from the unskilled to the semi-skilled grades, the women have in many cases taken their place on unskilled work, though many women have, of course, been employed on semi-skilled, and even on skilled, jobs. The unskilled women and girls hold their position in the vital industries only precariously, and are unlikely to count for much as a separate factor. They must be considered and provided for; but this will be done mainly by measures common to both sexes. Men's and women's interests do not diverge in any important respect : the real gulf that needs bridging is the gulf between the skilled and the

less skilled workers. This, I believe, can and will be met
temporarily by mutual concession ; but it can only be
met permanently by the emergence of a broader spirit
and a more comprehensive form of organisation.

IV

The Plan of Action

We can now return from our necessarily long survey
of the conditions which exist in the engineering and shipbuilding industries, and endeavour to outline, at least
provisionally, a possible plan of action. We have seen
that the problem of getting control in industry presents
itself in a different way in those cases in which the industry
is, or can at once become, nationally owned, and in those
in which the continuance of private capitalism is, for the
time at least, inevitable. Where, as in the Post Office,
national (or municipal) ownership already exists, the
workers can concentrate on a strategy for assuming the
greatest amount of control and responsibility possible ;
where national ownership is " practical politics," they can
concentrate, as the miners and railwaymen are doing,
on a demand for national ownership and democratic
control on lines already suggested in this book. But,
where national ownership is not immediately practicable,
then any winning of partial control must involve a new
relationship to the private employer, and, to some extent,
a sharing of control with him. What we have said
already with regard to "social peace" and the Whitley
Reports makes it clear that this is a very different proposition from that which confronts the miners or the postal
workers.

Where, from this point of view, do the engineering and shipbuilding industries stand ? To some extent in all three groups. Any programme drawn up by the workers in these industries must treat them, not as a whole, but as an agglomeration of distinct, though closely related, sections.

In the first group are the Royal Dockyards, Woolwich Arsenal, and the other establishments owned by the State. This is plain matter of fact, whereas the distinction between the second and third groups is a matter of opinion. I shall place unhesitatingly in the second group, that is to say, on a largely similar footing to mines and railways, first the whole of the shipbuilding industry, and secondly at least the central processes of armament manufacture. In the third group, as not immediately susceptible of nationalisation, I should place the general mass of the engineering industry and of the lesser metal trades connected with it.

I do not mean that the strategy to be followed by Labour in each of these groups is different in all, or in most, respects, but only that there are certain essential differences which must be appreciated at the outset. Thus, in the Royal Dockyards and Arsenals, the organised workers can press on with the policy of " encroaching control " without any fear of being drawn into an entanglement or *liaison* with private capitalism. This simplifies their problem immensely. The shipbuilding workers, on the other hand, ought, in my view, at once to formulate a scheme for the public ownership and democratic control of the shipbuilding industry, and ought to direct their principal energies to securing the adoption of this scheme. The time is more than ripe for a Shipbuilding Commission.

The body of workers in general engineering is in yet

another position. It has to reconcile itself to the continuance for a time of private ownership of the industry, and therefore its energies must be devoted on the one hand to winning as much power and control as it can, and on the other hand to refusing any form of " joint control " or " co-management " which would have the effect of entangling it with private capitalism. The additional temporary strategy of the shipyard workers—what they need to do in addition to scheming for public ownership with democratic control—will largely coincide with the strategy of general engineering workers ; and there will be a large field for a strategy common to all three groups, especially in the setting in order of their own Trade Union houses. In attempting to give body to this outline, I shall begin with the third group, that of general engineering, and then try to state more clearly the differences required for the other two groups.

Clearly in view of the disorganisation which has been described, the first necessity is an effective consolidation of Trade Union forces. This, I believe, in view of the present cleavage between skilled and less skilled workers, will have to come in a somewhat unsatisfactory way. First, there will need to be a fusion of the Unions representing mainly the various classes of skilled workers—engineers, smiths, electricians, moulders, pattern-makers and the rest. Of this, a beginning, but only a beginning, is being made by the engineering amalgamation that is now in progress. Similarly, there will have to be amalgamation into one Union of the various Unions of less skilled workers. This process has already begun, and an effective Federation, including most of the Societies, exists in the National Federation of General Workers. I want all the workers in the industry to be in one Union ; but for the present I want each of these groups to combine its own forces and then to fix up the closest possible working arrangement with the other.

On the side of the skilled Trade Unions, there is one thing which is hardly less important for the improvement of Trade Union machinery than amalgamation itself. This is the internal structure and government of the new Union which results from the amalgamation. If the rules and structure of the new body resemble those of the Unions of which it will be composed, then there is indeed little hope that it will be a powerful influence towards the winning of industrial control. Engineering Trade Unionism needs a " New Model " essentially different from the old "New Model " of seventy years ago, to which the existing Societies, on the whole, still scrupulously adhere. What is the essential new form of organisation that is required ?

The acid test of any new or revised Trade Union constitution in the engineering industry will be the recognition which it accords to organisation in the workshop. The workshop should be made the essential unit upon which the larger areas and authorities in the industry should be built up. Thus, the shop steward, and the right of the members in any shop to appoint shop stewards, must not merely be recognised, but treated as the first condition of effective organisation. The shop stewards must be given real duties and real powers, and in every works and shop there must be provision for regular meetings of the members and for the election of shop committees and a works committee, composed entirely of Trade Unionists, and properly representative of each grade and of each department. These committees, moreover, must be given full authority to co-operate with the shop and works representatives of the less skilled workers and of all workers who are in other recognised Unions.

The Works Committees in each factory, moreover, must be recognised not merely for " works " negotiation, but as constituent elements for the larger organisation of the District Committee, which should consist largely, if not entirely, of chief stewards chosen by the workers in the various factories. Thus, the whole district organisation of the Union for industrial purposes should be firmly placed upon a workshop basis.[1]

The works meetings and the Works Committees, co-ordinated by a District Committee mainly representative of them, would thus become the centres of the local activities of the Union. The next stage, I believe, should be a scheme of regional organisation under a number of regional committees, each representing the various district committees within its area, and covering a wide field. For instance, the North-East Coast (including the Tyne, Sunderland, Hartlepool, Middlesborough and other districts) would be one region, the West Riding of Yorkshire another, Lancashire and Cheshire a third, and so on.

Finally, for the national control of policy, I believe the best bodies to be, first, an executive consisting of a representative from each region, with a small nucleus of full-time permanent members who would form a standing committee; and, secondly, a National Conference, similar to those of the miners, drawn from every district in the Union. Such a constitution, I believe, would have the flexibility which is so urgently required. Its supreme merit would be that it would rest firmly upon a workshop basis, and that upon

[1] The existing Trade Union branches, which in most cases do not represent a real industrial unit at all, would thus be relieved of the industrial work of the Union, and would remain in being as centres of its "friendly society" activities.

the workshop all the larger authorities in it would be built up.

What would such a Union be able to accomplish in the direction of securing control ? It would be but an instrument, and our next task is that of showing how it could be employed. To a greater extent than in any other great industry, the problems of engineering are workshop problems. Although standardisation has made big advances, the immense diversity of engineering products, machinery, and methods of production means that the questions which arise between employers and workmen, apart from general questions of basic rates of wages, hours and conditions, arise very largely in the workshops themselves. This applies particularly to the most burning questions in the industry to-day—the manning of machines, payment by results, and scientific management. Round these questions the principal battles in the industry have for years past been joined, and it is not too much to say that whoever controls them has in his hand the key to the control of the industry itself, at least on its productive side. Upon winning control in this sphere, therefore, the engineers need to concentrate, and this makes workshop organisation the thing that is for them of primary importance.

Works and workshop organisation ought, throughout the industry, to be consciously directed to winning control of machines and their management.[1] Shop stewards ought to be purposefully selected, and accorded facilities for training, with this end in view. That is to say, the shop steward ought to be, in a certain measure, an industrial

[1] I have discussed a number of these problems, and the strategy to be adopted in winning control, much more fully in my book, *The Payment of Wages*, than I am able to discuss them here.

expert, and the Union ought to have in its service experts who could be called in to help the workers in effective negotiation with the employers. If the stewards assumed these functions and became possessed of the capacity and training required for them, big changes might be built upon their action.

Their constant and their main endeavour should be to substitute as far as possible for the individual relation of the employer, or his agent, with each worker, a collective relation of the employer with the whole of the workers employed in a particular shop or works. Instead of dealing with the firm individually, they ought to deal with it collectively. Let us take as examples four respects in which this change might be made.

At present, the employer engages and dismisses each workman individually. Already, his liberty in this respect it is to some extent limited by refusals of Trade Unionists to work with non-Union labour or to stomach unjust dismissals. But this process can be carried very much further. Why should not the workers in the shop, through their Shop Committee, engage all necessary labour and make all necessary dismissals ?

Secondly, at present the employer appoints foremen and supervisors to order the workers about. Here, again, his liberty is to some extent restrained by the refusal of Trade Unionists to work under particular foremen. But why should not the workers collectively choose their own " foremen," and undertake themselves to maintain the necessary order in the shop without interference from outside ?

Thirdly, at present the employer pays each worker individually. He cannot pay what rates he likes, for his liberty is restrained by Trade Union collective bargaining.

But why should not the Works Committee or the Shop Committee arrange with the employer for a lump payment to be made by him to the Committee, to be disbursed by it among the workers in the shop or works ?   This might be either a collective time-work payment, or a collective payment based on the total output of the shop or works. Or, as the next paragraph will make clear, the difference between the two might disappear under the new conditions.

Fourthly, at present the employer, subject to collective bargaining, fixes the actual hours of work in the factory, and determines the short time or overtime to be worked. Here again his liberty is restricted by Trade Union regulation.   But why should not the Works Committee fix its own hours of labour ?   If it agreed with the employer for a certain output at a certain price, the workers, having completed this output, could go home.   They would thus fix their own hours, and be free to make arrangements among themselves as to holidays, time-off, works meetings or educational classes, and so on.

I firmly believe that this policy, which is coming to be known by the name of *Collective Contract*, is the right policy for Labour in the engineering industry, and in other industries where conditions are similar, to pursue.   A sign that it is on the right lines is that it has been conceived separately by different groups of workers and theorists, without any form of consultation.   It was first outlined in the discussions which preceded the formation of the National Guilds League in 1914.[1]   It was rediscovered, in a narrower but more explicit form, both by Messrs. Paton and Gallacher in their pamphlet on *Industrial*

[1] The " The Storrington document," in which the report of these discussions was embodied, gives most of the essential points.

Democracy, published by the Paisley Trades Council in 1917, and by the Industrial Research Group (subsequently the N.G.L. branch) at Weymouth, which issued a series of pamphlets urging it upon the Trade Union movement. For some years it has taken a regular place in the propaganda of the Guild Socialists.

The fundamental significance of this plan of action lies in the fact that it is directed not to the admission of the workers to the conjoint exercise of a common control with the employer, but to the transference of certain functions *completely* from the employer to the workers. It is thus strictly consistent with the criteria laid down in the last chapter, and directly opposite in method to the Whitley Reports. Wherever private capitalism remains in possession, the workers must concentrate upon encroachments of this sort, and must refuse to be drawn into schemes of " joint control," whatever specious immediate advantages they may seem to offer.[1]

This negative side of the policy required for the workers in the engineering industry is hardly less important than its positive side. Proposals of profit-sharing or so-called "co-partnership " they must reject, even if the employer offers to share profits or control with the Union or the Works Committee and not with each individual employee. For any such scheme would tie them up with private capitalism and prevent them from developing a complete system of industrial self-government in the service of the whole community. This does not mean that there must be no joint committees of employers and employed. Such committees will be necessary as long as capitalism continues ;

[1] For a full discussion of this vital difference, see the chapter on "The Abolition of the Wage-System," in my *Self-Government in Industry.*

but they must be always bodies for negotiation between opposing forces, and never bodies for the joint and harmonious exercise of control. With the capitalists there is often an armistice, but there is never peace.

So far I have been speaking principally with reference to the general engineering group, which has not yet reached the stage at which immediate nationalisation becomes possible. With the necessary changes according to the slightly different character of the industry, what has been said applies equally to the shipyards as long as they remain under private ownership, and, as we shall see, to a great extent after they have become publicly owned. But the shipyard workers have also the duty of formulating a scheme for national ownership and democratic control, and such a scheme should, I think, follow very largely the same lines as the miners' scheme described above, except that, in the shipyards, the Yard Committees would be relatively more powerful and would have larger functions in relation to the District Councils than the Pit Committees would have in relation to the District Mining Councils. This, however, is a detail which does not affect the general character of the scheme.

If the shipyards were to be nationalised,[1] the problem of securing control in them would be to some extent affected by the progress which might have been made towards self-government in the Royal Dockyards. There has been, in the Dockyards, a growth of the Shop Stewards' movement parallel to the growth in private industry, and the whole policy of Collective Contract and encroaching control is equally applicable not only to engineering shops and private shipyards, but also to Government Dockyards and

[1] It should be observed that shipping requires to be nationalised together with shipbuilding.

Arsenals.   The difference arises only in relation to further steps, in addition to direct encroachments, which may be taken in the direction of control.   The application of the Whitley Report to the Dockyards, which has recently been carried into effect, will serve to illustrate my meaning.   In view of the fact that there can be in this case no possible danger of falling unawares into an alliance or compact with private capitalism, I not only see no objection to the acceptance of the Whitley scheme, under right conditions, in the dockyards, but certain positive advantages.   It must, however, be clearly understood that the Whitley scheme is not in any sense a substitute for encroaching control of the type described.   It is an additional method which may be valuable as facilitating the close co-operation of the workers of all grades, by hand and brain, and as enabling the Trade Unions to extend their control over wider questions of policy which cannot be dealt with by the workers in a single yard or department.   In publicly owned industries, many forms of "joint control" are possible and expedient, whereas they may be insidious dangers under private ownership.   But in no case can "joint control" of any sort be a substitute for encroaching control by means of the transference of specific functions to the workers themselves.

CHAPTER IX

SOME " DIFFICULT " INDUSTRIES—TEXTILES AND BUILDING

I

THE TEXTILE INDUSTRIES

THE textile group of industries, of which the cotton industry is in this country by far the most important, forms, next to the metal group with which we have been dealing, by far the largest group connected with large-scale factory production. In certain important respects the conditions in the textile group are essentially different from those which exist in engineering and ship-building, and call for a somewhat different strategy on the part of the workers in forwarding their demand for control. If we can see clearly a line of policy for the Trade Unions in one of the industries belonging to this textile group, we shall have gone far towards defining a policy for large-scale factory industries as a whole ; for the remaining industries will, to a great extent, fall between the two extremes, and require a strategy approximating either to the one or to the other.

What, then, is the principal difference that clearly distinguishes the greater part of the textile group from the greater part of engineering and shipbuilding? [1] It is at present

[1] The iron and steel industry is in some respects closer to the textile industries than to engineering and shipbuilding.

this. Despite the advance in standardised production in the engineering group, a very high proportion of its work still approximates to "individual" rather than to "mass" production. Its problems are thus very largely workshop problems, arising in a particular works, and in relation to a particular worker or group of workers. Thus, where systems of payment by results are in operation, piece-work prices or bonus times are, in the engineering industry, fixed in the great majority of cases within a particular shop or even for a particular job. To some extent such methods of price-fixing are still found in the less organised sections of the textile industries ; but wherever organisation has become strong, and especially in the cotton industry, price-fixing has been made the subject of elaborate collective bargains, applying not to a particular factory, but over a large area, or even over the industry as a whole. These bargains have taken shape in elaborate standard price-lists, to which almost the whole of the firms in the industry have to conform. This has happened because of the nature of the work done, and not because of a peculiar caprice on the part of the persons concerned. Textile factory production has become a pure "repetition job," the pace of which is largely set by the machine. The output, unlike that in the greater part of the engineering industry, is readily susceptible of exact measurement, which does roughly correspond to the amount of effort and skill expended in production. Collective bargaining by the Trade Unions on a basis far wider than that of the single factory, has therefore been able to establish itself as the normal method of determining remuneration on a piece-work basis.[1]

[1] For a much fuller explanation of this contract and of its effects, see my *Payment of Wages*, especially chapters iv. and xi.

The consequences of this repetitive character of the work and of the Trade Union methods resulting from it are seen in the temper of the workers employed. The outside observer is often puzzled by the fact that the Shop Stewards' movement, while it has firmly established itself in the engineering industry, has hitherto made little headway in the textile industries, despite repeated attempts by the "left wing" to get it into operation. But surely the reason is obvious and lies in the different characters of the two groups. Workshop problems are always arising in the average engineering shop, and will continue to arise until and unless the engineering industry has become as completely standardised and mechanised as the cotton industry is to-day. This is not to say that there are no workshop or factory problems in the cotton industry. There are such problems, arising, for instance, out of questions of faulty material, bad spinning, lack of factory amenities, or bad ventilation. But these problems are not nearly so numerous or so likely to give rise to an active workshop movement as the problems of engineering shop practice. In the cotton industry, most of the work necessarily falls upon the district Trade Union officials, whereas in engineering a great deal falls upon the actual workers in the shop.

This fact largely accounts for the notable "apathy" of and lack of constructive aspirations among the rank and file workers in the textile industries. There is very little in the nature of their working conditions to rouse them to active participation in the affairs of their Union or their industry. It also largely accounts for the lack of "ginger" among the Trade Union officials ; for the price-list method of payment tends to reduce these officials to expert calculating machines and to knock out of their heads all ideas of real economic democracy.

The textile workers bore the brunt of the Industrial Revolution, and at the present time they bear its marks and scars upon them more plainly than any other class. They are the " damaged goods " of capitalism, and the damage they have suffered is a fact of which the constructive revolutionary is bound to take account. The road to control is a far harder road to tread for the workers in the cotton industry than for the groups of which we have hitherto spoken, and the very conditions under which the industry is conducted make the workers less capable and less desirous of setting foot upon it.

The cotton industry has to a great extent lost the predominant position which it once occupied in the Trade Union movement. While the chief struggle centred round rates of wages and the securing of rudimentary legal protection by means of the Factory Acts, the peculiar handicaps under which the textile workers now suffer did not matter ; for the problems were then problems to be tackled for the industry as a whole, and not for any particular factory. But, as soon as the idea of industrial democracy was born and the claim for the control of industry by the workers began to be put forward, cotton dropped out of the front rank and fell back to the very rear of the Trade Union movement. During the last few years, there have been several attempts to secure the adoption in the cotton industry of the system of shop stewards and works committees ; but these attempts have so far been purely local, and have not yet affected the industry as a whole.[1]

What, then, is, for textile operatives in general, and for cotton operatives in particular, the road to control ?   The

[1] Similar isolated attempts have been made in the boot and shoe (factory) industry, to which most of what has been said about the textile industries applies with equal force.

cotton industry at least, in Lancashire and the adjoining
counties, is well organised so far as numbers are concerned.
The various sections are indeed divided one from another,
and the method of craft organisation still prevails. On
the " preparing " side of the industry, the Card and Blow-
ing Room Operatives' Amalgamation and the Spinners'
Amalgamation (which still excludes the unfortunate
assistants, the piecers, from any real share in its control)
contain the bulk of the membership ; while, on the manufacturing side, the Amalgamations of Weavers, Overlookers,
Tapesizers, Warpdressers, Beamers, Twisters and Drawers,
and Warehousemen are in a similar position. The Bleachers
and Dyers have their own separate organisation. These
bodies are federated in various ways, most but not all
belonging to a big " consultative " Federation, the United
Textile Factory Workers' Association, which does not
itself negotiate, and is rather a debating Congress and a
political body than an effective industrial Federation.[1]

This central association has recently been showing certain
signs of life and of the desire for a forward policy, and has
begun to discuss the project of national ownership of the
cotton industry. Until quite recently, this proposal was
not seriously discussed, and was hardly even taken seriously
at all. The very high profits realised by the industry during
the last few years, and the fever of speculation in mill shares
which began to visit Lancashire immediately after the
conclusion of the war, had a powerful effect upon the
workers' minds, and induced them to turn their attention
to national ownership as a possible remedy. They saw

[1] There is a separate body, the Northern Counties Textile
Trades Federation, which unites fairly effectively most of the
Societies on the manufacturing side of the industry, but does
not include either the Spinners or the Cardroom Operative.

that the hugely increased capitalisation which resulted from these share transactions and from the floating of new companies meant a vastly increased expectation of profits from the industry, and that to pay 5 per cent on the new capital values might mean that the firm would have to " earn," with the same plant and the same number of workers, 20 or 30 per cent on the old values. This, they saw, would place a vast new obstruction in the way of improvements in wages and conditions, which had always been low and bad owing to the pressure of foreign competition, despite the completeness of Trade Union organisation. A demand for the nationalisation of the cotton industry is therefore beginning to be made with some vigour.

It will be seen at once that the pushing of such a demand will create a new industrial situation. Although Socialists and Trade Unionists have again and again declared for the nationalisation of "the means of production, distribution and exchange," there has been something a trifle academic about this pronouncement, and the cases in which nationalisation has been pressed forward as a practical policy for immediate adoption have been those of great public utilities, such as mines and railways. The claim for the nationalisation of the cotton industry would be a demand which would set a new precedent in practical politics.

Nevertheless, I believe that this demand is one which the workers in the cotton industry ought to put forward with all the force at their disposal. To concentrate entirely upon the endeavour to create an effective workshop movement similar to that which has come into existence in the engineering industry would be to embark on a very long and painful process, under conditions which present almost insuperable difficulties. The attempt to create and to render effective a workshop movement in the cotton industry must indeed be made, but I believe that it will be greatly facilitated by the simultaneous presentation of a demand for nationalisation. Such a demand must, of course, be couched in similar terms to that of the miners, and must include democratic control as well as national ownership.

Here we at once encounter the central difficulty. In the cotton industry, the manufacturing processes, including preparing as well as manufacture in the narrower sense, have been largely reduced to routine. Managerial and technical skill in the industry are to a great extent concentrated at its two " business " ends, so that, in the national economy, cotton appears less as a group of manufacturing processes than as a group of commercial processes tied together by certain processes of manufacture. It is the purchase of raw cotton, with all the speculation which centres round the Liverpool Cotton Exchange, at the one end, and the sale of cotton goods, with all the complications of the shipping and export trade, at the other, that constitute the real problems as soon as the nationalisation of the cotton industry is suggested.

Two questions are thus raised. First, the workers in the industry itself have little or no knowledge of these processes, and this applies to a great extent even to the technical and managerial staffs connected with the factory side of the industry. They cannot therefore effectively control, or claim to control, these operations. If, then, the cotton industry is nationalised, the control of these commercial operations will have, in the main, to be left to the State. This at once raises the second question : Is the State at present capable of assuming the management of these complex operations of commerce, which have necessitated the evolution of highly specialised classes of business men ?

The difficulty of dealing with the export trade has often been raised as an objection to the nationalisation of the coal industry. But the problem of coal exports is a mere fleabite in comparison with the twofold problem presented by the commercial operations of the cotton industry. To leave these operations in private hands while nationalising manufacture would be useless : to nationalise them seems at present almost impossible.

Nothing that I am saying is meant to cast a doubt upon the practicability of cotton nationalisation at a later stage. I believe that the commercial operations in the purchase of raw cotton could be to a great extent eliminated, and that the complexity of the export trade could be greatly reduced, and that nationalisation could thus be made a perfectly practicable proposition. If the Cotton Control scheme which existed during the war [1] had been developed along proper lines and made permanent, it could have been used to make nationalisation a practicable policy. Probably the fear of this was the principal reason for its precipitate abandonment at the earliest possible moment. A transitional period of control over the commercial side of the industry is probably an indispensable preliminary to national ownership. It is a thousand pities that the cotton Trade Union leaders did not realise this, and cling to and develop the very embryonic form of control which was secured under the stress of war conditions.

[1] For a full account of this scheme and its possibilities, and also of the more developed Wool Control Scheme, see *Past and Future*, by " Jason." The National Guilds League, at its Annual Conference in May 1918, carried a resolution advocating the policy here outlined, while recognising the possible dangers attaching to such a system of capitalist State control.

In view of the facts which I have outlined, it seems very improbable that nationalisation of the cotton industry can be secured at once. This, however, is not a reason why the Trade Unions should not begin at once to agitate for it, and to urge, as a preparatory measure, the imposition of effective State control, in which the Unions would participate, as they did during the war, over commercial operations connected with the industry, with a view to the elimination of speculation and of unnecessary complications. This is not the place to deal with the wider question of the control of export trade under industrial democracy. It is a vast problem, which urgently needs fuller treatment than I can give to it in this chapter.

To press for nationalisation and control, with full Trade Union participation, over the commercial side of the cotton industry, is not, of course, enough. At the same time, the Trade Unions must endeavour to improve their organisation, and to adopt a policy which will give them encroaching control over the factory side. We have seen the difficulties which face them in this sphere ; but it is manifest that, if there is to be industrial democracy at all, these difficulties must be overcome. What, then, are the measures which it is possible to suggest ?

First, and obviously, the existing sectionalism ought to disappear by the amalgamation of the various Unions into a single Union covering the industry as a whole. Such a Union should take full account of the differences between the preparing and manufacturing sections, and between the various grades in these sections, and should provide for grade representation and sectional autonomy in grade and sectional affairs. This reorganisation should be accompanied by an overhauling of the internal machinery of the cotton Trade Unions, with a view to a better selection of officials not exclusively or mainly for the expert job of price-list bargaining, which has resulted in a general narrowing of outlook, but for all the various functions which have to be performed in the industry.   Specialisation is necessary ; but it is very bad economy for all the officials to specialise on the same thing, and in the cotton Trade Unions they have hitherto been forced to do so by the extreme sectionalism and localisation of the various societies.

With the re-creation of Trade Unionism on a wider basis must go an attempt, even in face of the difficulties, to stimulate an active Trade Union organisation in each mill.   As we have seen, the fact that negotiations and disputes about piece-work prices and methods of remuneration generally cover an area much wider than that of the single mill, tends to remove the most active stimulus to workshop organisation from within the mill itself.   It is therefore not very likely that an effective Mill Stewards' movement will arise in the cotton industry, as the Shop Stewards' movement arose in engineering, by the spontaneous creation of the rank and file, and even apart from the stimulus of a clearly realised purpose.   A Mill Stewards' movement, though it will be aided by sporadic rank and file movements, will have to come mainly as the result of deliberate creation by the Trade Unions themselves, and the most essential first step is therefore the conversion of the Trade Unions to an understanding of the necessity for such a movement.

It would be useless to create a Mill Stewards' movement unless, when it had been created, there would be definite work for it to do—work which would appeal to the mill operatives and make them conscious of the need for keeping the mill movement alive and active.   A mill movement which had to be constantly stimulated and "gingered up" by the Trade Unions, would obviously have in it no principle of vitality. What, then, would be the driving force behind the movement, if it could once be called into effective existence ?

Clearly, it could not centre nearly so much as the engineering movement round questions such as payment by results, or the manning of machines. It would therefore have to concentrate in the first instance rather on the wider questions of the conditions of labour than on the narrower problems of remuneration. It would, indeed, have to deal with the " remuneration " questions of faulty material, " bad spinning," etc., which have been mentioned already ; but these would be only a small part of its work, and would provide an altogether inadequate basis for an active movement.

The key to the problem seems to me to lie partly in the sphere of what is sometimes called " welfare." Trade Unionists hate the name because it has come to stand for a form of " paternal " and often self-interested provision made by the employer, and under the employer's control. But employers' " welfare " has invaded the factories only because the Trade Unions have been neglectful of the problem of conditions of labour. In the textile industry, these are of very great importance. The sanitary conditions and discomfort of the mills are in many cases appalling. The Factory Acts are almost obsolete as methods of protection, and it is high time for the Trade Unions, through mill stewards and mill committees, to take up the task of protecting their own members, and of making the factories, as far as possible, fit places in which to work.

I am not suggesting that the control of " welfare " by

the workers, or rather the democratic safeguarding of the conditions of labour, is an end in itself, or more than a very preliminary step, among other steps, towards getting a Mill Stewards' movement on its feet. When that has been done, the policy of " collective contract " [1] follows as it follows upon the successful creation of the Shop Stewards' movement in the engineering industry. But it is useless to talk about " collective contract " and " encroaching control " until there is a definite movement and organisation actually in being in the factory, and therefore the first need is to take the measures which will be successful in bringing such an organisation into effective existence.

" Encroaching control " is for cotton operatives as for other classes of workers the principal method of emancipation. Even if the methods of remuneration continue to be determined outside the factory on the basis of price-lists arranged by the Union as a whole, this does not preclude the adoption of the policy if once a nucleus can be formed round which mill organisation can gather. It is no less necessary and possible for the cotton operatives than for the engineering workers to secure collective control over engagements and dismissals, over the appointment of overlookers and managers, over the distribution of pay, and over the actual hours of work, and the organisation of the workshop as a whole. The movement in the mills, if once it can get an effective start on the right lines, will grow spontaneously into a movement capable of exercising control.

I have spoken throughout the chapter mainly of the cotton industry, which is, in this country, the most important in the textile group. Most of what has been said

[1] See pp. 154 ff.

applies also to the wool industry of the West Riding, and to the minor textile industries principally carried on in the Midlands and in Scotland and Ireland. These are, as a rule, far less highly organised on both sides, and have far less developed methods of collective bargaining—a fact which, in some ways, will probably make it easier to build up an effective mill movement among the wool operatives of Yorkshire than among the cotton workers. But, whatever may be the minor differences or the differences of degree, the broad policy outlined above seems to hold good for all. Probably wool and cotton will have to lead the way, unless the cotton and wool dyeing trade, which is well organised and, owing to the character of its processes, admirably adapted for a strong workshop movement, becomes the pioneer. At present, it must be confessed that the textile industries show lamentably few signs of readiness to play an effective part in the forward movement of Labour. They are crusted with conservatism and bowed beneath the long-borne load of large-scale production. This section is an attempt to suggest a possible policy for their awakening, accompanied by a full realisation of the difficulties with which they are confronted. A clear understanding of these difficulties is the necessary condition of any effective attempt at their removal.

II

The Building Industry

It has long been obvious—long even before the war —that the British building industry stands in need of reconstruction. It is not technically efficient ; its methods have been unprogressive and it has rubbed along somehow without any system of costing or scientific pricing of jobs ; it has been peculiarly liable to dislocation and to ups and downs of employment which have had a bad effect on the working personnel ; it has been under-capitalised and overstocked with small masters ; it has suffered from a lack of contact between architect and builder, and the architect has suffered because he has been forced to become less a designer than an engineer and quantity surveyor. The personnel of the industry —designer, surveyor, employer, and workman alike— have suffered severely from a lack of imagination, and have persisted in conservative courses even when their serious effects upon the industry had become manifest.

The years before the war were, of course, years of depression in the building industry. The war, while it caused a certain amount of emergency building in munitions areas, virtually shut down private building altogether. In consequence of the housing shortage thus created, and of the growing demand for a higher standard of accommodation in houses, schools and buildings generally, there can be no question of a shortage of work for a long time to come. Builders are certain to be busy and prosperous ; it is only a question of how the industry is to be organised in order to give better service to the public than it has given in the past.

In order to understand the developments which are now being discussed, it is necessary to realise that, outside of London and a very few other of the largest towns, there are hardly any large employers in the industry. The great bulk of the work is in the hands either of a very small number of big contractors, or of a very large number of quite small masters. The London Master Builders' Association, which has conducted such fierce campaigns

against trade unionism in the past, is predominantly
representative of the big employers; the numerous
associations in the provinces mostly represent quite small
employers.

These small employers, who are thus still the largest
factor in the industry, usually combine in their own
persons the rôles of capitalists and managers. The
amount of capital required for the smaller building operations is very little, and the normal master in the industry
is a comparatively poor man, using a small amount of
capital, whether borrowed or his own, and usually managing
his own business, often by methods which are largely
those of rule of thumb.

Almost all the associations of building trade employers,
including the London as well as the provincial associations,
are represented on a National Federation, while the
operatives, on their side, have a National Federation
which includes nearly all the trades in England and Wales,
though it does not effectively cover Scotland. Between
these two federations has been established the Building
Trades Parliament, officially known as the National
Industrial Council for the Building Industry.

This joint body, representing employers and Trade
Unions, has for some time been considering the whole
future of the building industry. It appointed a committee, nominally to deal with scientific management
and reduction of costs, and the first report of this Committee was submitted to a full meeting of the Building
Trades Parliament on 14th August 1919. It must be
remembered that it is the report of a joint committee of
eight employers and eight trade unionists, not, indeed,
unanimously agreed to, but concurred in by a majority
of the Committee, and ordered to be placed before the

full body. It is a remarkable document, and the most remarkable thing about it is that it emanates from an industry which has been, hitherto, so little inclined to self-examination of any sort.

It is clear that, as soon as the Committee set out to deal with scientific management and cost of production, they saw the impossibility of making any changes that would be effective without submitting to the most searching examination the very principles, or lack of principles, upon which the industry is at present conducted. They saw that, on the one hand, the employer is often unimaginative and hampered by insecurity and lack of capital ; while, on the other hand, the workers are subject to recurrent periods of unemployment and disinclined to take any special trouble while the industry is conducted for private profit and they have no control over its working. With these and similar unpleasant facts in mind, the Committee set to work to lay down a basis on which the industry might not merely free itself of the difficulties which drag it down, but become organised to a real and considerable extent on the basis of public service.

Beginning with the workers, the Committee suggested in the first place that a levy of, at the most, 5 per cent on the wages bills of all employers would suffice to give every Trade Unionist in the industry an absolute guarantee against unemployment. They did not, indeed, suggest that full wages should be paid to the unemployed worker, but half wages, supplemented by a payment of 10 per cent for the wife and the same payment for each child under sixteen years of age, up to a maximum of full wages. This unemployment provision, to be dispensed by the Trade Unions and paid over to them as a charge on the industry, was not to be called upon until every effort had been made to decasualise building work and open up avenues of steady employment. For this purpose local, regional and national joint committees of employers and trade unionists were to be set up, to work in the closest possible conjunction with public authorities and other customers or clients of the building industry. The Committee anticipated that the guarantee against the rigours incidental to unemployment would clear away one of the most powerful obstacles to the active co-operation of the worker in making the industry as efficient and successful as possible.

But the scheme propounded by the Committee goes very much further than that. It was realised that, if the operatives' status needs to be changed, so also does that of the employer. It was therefore proposed to discriminate sharply between " capital " and " management." The real capital employed in the industry, it was proposed, should be ascertained, and on this real capital should be paid a guaranteed and limited rate of interest, varying with the yield on Government securities. The services of management should also be ascertained, and each employer who is also a manager should receive, as manager, an adequate salary. In short, he should cease to be an employer in the ordinary sense, whatever he might remain in name, and should become the servant of the industry as a whole.

Varying profits, as distinguished from fixed interest on capital and remuneration for management, disappear under this scheme. It is anticipated that, even after guaranteeing reasonable interest on capital, except where the failure to earn the interest could be shown to be the result of mismanagement, there would certainly remain a surplus in the hands of the industry. This surplus, it was proposed, should be used not for distribution to owners or managers, but for the benefit of the industry, for the provision of new capital as required, for superannuation, and for other communal purposes of the industry. The employer would thus remain in the industry in his capacity of manager, and the desire to amass huge profits at the expense of the consumer would, it was contended, become obsolete.

If the element of capital could be, as it were, "segregated" and assured of neither more nor less than a moderate fixed return ; if the employer became a manager, and his gain, varying from ability or by luck, were replaced by a salary varying with his competence and scale of operations ; if the manual worker received an assured status in the industry by being relieved of the fear of unemployment and secured, through works committees and local and national committees, a real share in control, then, it is urged, the way would be clear for a real reformation of building enterprise as a whole. The ideal of public service would be able to assume its rightful place, and the profit-making motive would be dethroned.

Of course, much would still remain to be done. The present building trade employers and the manual workers are by no means the whole personnel of the industry. The architect has also to be considered, and here it must be admitted that the proposed scheme of reorganisation was sadly deficient. It was indeed intended to allow a single architect, nominated by his professional association, to sit upon the joint committee which it was proposed to establish locally between the building industry and the public authorities. But beyond this, the imagination of the Committee responsible for the scheme does not appear to have carried them. They presented no vision of the architect as an integral part of the industry, who must be absorbed into and assured of his rightful place in the structure before the health of the industry can be restored. This omission is, no doubt, largely the result of circumstances beyond the control of those who drew up the scheme. In the Building Trades Parliament they found ready to their hands joint machinery in which manual workers and employers were already associated together, and they well knew that neither side on this body would be prepared to tolerate the intrusion into it of the architects as a third party while the existing relations between employers and workers remained on their present footing. It is, however, fairly clear that, if some scheme such as that which the Committee proposed were successfully carried out, it would make far easier the incorporation of the architect, in his function as designer and planner, into the structure of the industry, because the industry would have become less a battleground for two contending parties.

But the scheme had a defect even greater than its failure to provide for the incorporation of the architect, and a defect which is more serious, because it could have been more easily remedied. This is its failure to provide for a real development of workshop self-government. Such a development is not, indeed, wholly inconsistent with the scheme ; but it is not provided for, probably because there would have been little hope of persuading the majority of employers to agree to it. In speaking of the Whitley Reports and of the general strategy of encroaching control, we have seen that no form of joint organisation can under any conceivable conditions take the place of an actual encroachment by the workers, or of the assumption by them of a measure of exclusive control, even if it be within a restricted sphere.

The building industry is by its nature admirably adapted for the application of such a policy of encroachment as the past experiments in " direct labour " under

12

collective control have amply sufficed to demonstrate.
The building "job" forms an admirable natural unit
round which a policy of collective contract can be built
up. It differs from the workshop in that it is not a permanent, but a constantly changing unit, and there will
be consequential changes in the form of job organisation
and in the relation of job organisation to the Trade
Unions ; but clearly the possibility of real industrial
democracy in the building industry depends on the success
with which "job" organisation is fostered by the Trade
Unions and developed by them into a full system of
collective control of labour and of the job.

Where the need for the policy of encroaching control
is realised, a difference still arises as to the strategy to be
followed. Some will say that the right policy is to cut
the employer out of the industry altogether, and for the
Union to offer to supply the whole of the labour required
for the job, including the supervision and organisation,
the purchaser, whether it be a public body or a private
person, supplying the materials, and, for the present at
least, probably also employing the architect. Under this
plan, the idea is that the employer should be frozen out,
or only allowed to come back as a salaried manager
engaged by the Trade Union itself.

The alternative suggestion is an extension of the proposal
contained in the Report of the Builders' Parliament. It
is urged that the workers should demand and obtain
collective control of their own labour and of the job as
they would under the first scheme ; but that the employer
should remain, with the changed semi-managerial status
advocated in the Report, and should continue to be
responsible for the provision of materials and plant.
This also involves the continuance of the payment of a

guaranteed but limited rate of interest on the actual capital invested in the industry.

The choice between these two alternatives does not seem to me to be absolute, so far as the immediate policy to be adopted is concerned. I favour the method of direct labour, including management and organisation, provided and controlled by the Trade Unions, wherever it can be put into force. But I do not regard it as generally practicable at once, although it should become increasingly easy as Labour pursues its conquest of the local authorities, which for some time to come will certainly be the chief consumers of the products of the building industry. This method should then be extended as rapidly as possible ; but side by side with it there is room for experiments on different lines. We shall most easily see what these can be if we examine the reception accorded to the proposals put forward by the special committee of the Builders' Parliament.

The Report described above drew its chief inspiration from Mr. Malcolm Sparkes, formerly an employer in the building trade, and virtually the founder of the Builders' Parliament itself. It was agreed to by the whole of the eight Trade Unionists on the Committee, but by only three out of the eight employers. When it came before the full Builders' Parliament, the reference back of the whole Report was moved from the employers' side. This, however, was heavily defeated, a considerable number of employers voting with the Trade Unionists against it. A resolution was then adopted, not accepting the Report, but instructing the same Committee to proceed to a further and more detailed consideration of the problems involved. As I write, this further consideration is in progress, and all the indications point to the conclusion that the new Report will be much more far-reaching than the first. It will probably include, first, a " compulsory code " for the industry as a whole, centering round the guarantee against unemployment suggested in the Interim Report; but it will include also a " voluntary code," which will be practically a proposal for the constitution on voluntary lines of a National Guild of Builders, to be formed by the operatives' Federation, to which master builders will be asked to adhere, the Guild being prepared to purchase their property at a fair valuation and to offer to competent employers positions as managers under the Guild.

It was clear from the reception accorded to the first Report that there was no chance that it would be adopted as a whole by the industry as a whole.   Before the whole body of employers would accept it, it would have to be so whittled down as to be valueless as a step towards industrial democracy.   Its only chance therefore lay in its voluntary adoption, or in the voluntary adoption of a better scheme incorporating the necessary provisions for workers' control of labour and of the job, by a minority of employers acting in conjunction with the Trade Unions concerned. If the necessary provision for democratic control of the job is made, I can see substantial advantages in such a partial adoption of it not as an alternative to, but side by side with, a steady extension of the method of direct workers' control already outlined.   This latter method will find its chief field for operation in the execution of public contracts, while the " joint " scheme would probably operate mainly in fulfilling private demands.

The position of the building industry differs considerably in several respects from the position of the industries which we have previously been considering in this book. It is not a " factory " but a " job " industry, and the labour groups which it creates are, apart from the workshop production which is incidental to it, temporary rather than permanent groups. It is, from the point of view of economic structure, still for the most part a small-scale industry, including comparatively few large employers apart from the vast contracting firms. Its labour is migratory in a quite unusual degree. All these and other characteristics mark it out for separate treatment, while its manual character and retention of a high degree of craft possibilities should make it an admirable field for experiments in the Guild direction. A few years ago, building Trade Unionism seemed to be plunged in complete apathy; but a big awakening is in progress, and probably the chief use of the Industrial Parliament's Report is that it has stimulated discussion, and caused Trade Unionists to endeavour to formulate a constructive policy for themselves. It is too early as yet to prophesy the direction which the movement will take; but I have little doubt that, in one way or another, building will yet prove a " key " industry in the evolution of industrial self-government.

NOTE.—This Chapter was already in the printer's hands before the Manchester building operatives launched their plan for a Building Guild, and before I had heard of any such intention. It will be seen, however, that the proposal which I put forward tallies almost exactly with the methods adopted by the Manchester operatives, with the help of that " father of National Guilds," Mr. S. G. Hobson. As the Manchester scheme has at once raised the issue in a concrete form, I now add to this Chapter a new section dealing with some of the difficulties which have been advanced.

III

The Building Guild

From time to time the idea of doing without capitalists or employers, and organising instead the work of
production on a basis of democratic self-government,
has caught hold more or less firmly of the working-
class. It was strongly present in the Owenite movement
in the 'thirties of the last century, and led them to the
formation of a Builders' Guild, whose ambitious projects
attracted for a time widespread public attention. This,
far more than the desire for co-operation of consumers,
was the ideal behind the earliest Co-operative Societies,
which regarded their business of buying and selling household goods for their members purely as a first step towards
the establishment of self-governing workshops. In a
slightly different form, the same idea came to the front
again in the middle of the century under the auspices of the
Christian Socialists, and some of the older producers'
co-operative factories which exist to-day owe their inception
to this movement. Of these attempts, the Builders' Guild
failed absolutely ; the Co-operative movement departed
from its original idea and built up its vast structure of
production and distribution on the basis of consumers',
instead of producers', co-operation ; and the producers'
societies, while many of them have survived and some
have done well, have shown their powerlessness to make
any breach in the fabric of capitalist industry, and have
mostly relied for their success on the possession of a de-
pendable market in the consumers' Co-operative movement.

Confronted with these failures, absolute or relative,

the idealists in the Labour movement who believe in producers' control have not abandoned their ideal, but have clothed it in a new form.   They have recognised definitely that the hope of success depends upon a clear realisation of two things—first, that any progress towards control must be based upon the Trade Union movement, and must have behind it the organised power and control over Labour, now approaching a monopoly, possessed by the Trade Unions ; and, secondly, that attempts by the workers to base their experiments upon capital provided by, or lent directly to, themselves are doomed to failure or insignificance.   The new demand, in the case of both miners and railwaymen—by whom it has been most clearly and definitely formulated—has therefore taken shape as a demand for a partnership in control between the workers by hand and brain and the public.   In these two cases, national ownership and democratic control by the workers form the substance of the demand.

The proposal put forward by the building workers of Manchester, and now being rapidly taken up in other districts, is, with certain differences, essentially based on the same principles as the demands of the miners and the railwaymen.   The differences arise chiefly from differences in the industries themselves.   Mines and railways are industries with an immense fixed capital, while in building the element of fixed capital is unimportant in comparison with the charges connected with each particular job.   Materials and labour are almost the whole costs of the building industry.   This fact makes it a case to which, if to any case, the idea of industrial self-government is easily applicable.   For whereas in mining the demand at once raises the issue of mine ownership and therefore involves nationalisation, in building there is

very little, unless goodwill is included, that can be nationalised or transferred to a public authority.

When, therefore, the building workers come forward
with an offer to form a Guild and to build, for a beginning,
2000 houses for the Manchester City Council, the question
of fixed capital and its ownership hardly arises, and the
only financial problem is that of credit, or of the provision
of the " floating capital " required to purchase the materials
and the necessary minimum of plant for the job.   If this
can be satisfactorily met, the remaining problems present
every appearance of simplicity.   It is a fact beyond dispute
that the Trade Unions concerned in the scheme do possess
a practical monopoly of labour, and that they are in a
position, as no one else is, to mobilise for the work of house-
building a sufficient supply of labour.   In view of the fact
that the great majority of building-trade operatives are at
present employed not on the urgent work of house-building
but on far less urgent, if commercially more profitable,
classes of work, the public clearly cannot afford to ignore
the monopoly of labour, with the consequent power of
mobilising it in the public service which the building Trade
Unions possess.   Indeed, at Irlam, not far from Manchester,
this issue has already been presented in the most concrete
of all possible forms.   The Irlam Council had before it rival
offers from the Trade Union Guild Committee and from the
local master builders.   The former was in a position to
ensure the requisite supply of labour ; the latter were not.
Here was one very strong card in the hand of the organised
workers, and its strength was speedily shown by the acceptance of the Guild offer by the Irlam District Council.[1]

[1] The Manchester City Council has not yet accepted the Guild
offer, which is still under discussion.   The Irlam acceptance still
awaits endorsement by the Ministry of Health (*March 1920*).

But—and this is the point that gives pause to the local Councils, accustomed only to commercial dealings of the ordinary type—is there an adequate answer to the financial criticism ? The Guild may be able to give a labour guarantee, but can it give a financial guarantee ? It is not enough to answer that the master builders, even if they can give a financial guarantee, cannot give a labour guarantee ; for the object is not only that of proving the unsoundness of their position, but that of demonstrating the soundness of the position of the Guild. What, then, is the Guild's answer on this point ? It refuses to give a financial guarantee in the ordinary sense, on the ground that it is based not on capital, but on labour. It does not say that its labour monopoly is a direct substitute for the master builders' possession of capital : it says that if its labour monopoly is united with the command of capital possessed by the local housing authority, nothing further is required in order to provide for the erection of houses on a perfectly sound business basis—different, indeed, from the basis of ordinary capitalist business, but far more sound. In other words, it urges the local authority to supply the money for the scheme, while it promises to supply the labour. It suggests a partnership between the producers and the public which is in its essentials, though not on the surface, the same as the partnership proposed by the miners.

It should be observed that the Guild will not be called upon to advance at the outset all the labour required to build 2000 houses, but only to give an assurance of its ability and readiness to do so. The labour-power will be supplied and expended gradually as the building proceeds. In the same way, the local authority is not called upon to advance at once all the money required for the building of 2000 houses, but only to give a parallel assurance, and, after a certain advance to set matters going, to supply money gradually as the work proceeds. The local authority is not called upon to stake on the success of the venture a huge sum of which it risks the loss if the venture fails. It is only called upon for gradual advances, and if the scheme breaks down at any point before completeness, it will have in its possession work done which roughly corresponds to the amount of money expended, and will be in as good a position as it is now to proceed with the building by other means.

So far from being an impracticable or visionary financial arrangement, this is precisely how a great deal of building was financed for many years before the war. A building syndicate acquired a site, and invited private builders to build upon it. These private builders in many cases had practically no financial resources, and the syndicate advanced them money, in small instalments, as the work proceeded, for the payment of their bills for materials and of their wages and other charges. Quite often these builders, from one cause or another, failed to complete ; but, so far from suffering serious losses, the syndicate was amply guarded, and sometimes did quite well out of their failure. We are far from suggesting that the local authorities should now borrow and apply the less reputable methods of the private building syndicate ; but, in face of these perfectly well-known facts, it does seem to us absurd to suggest that Guild building is impossible because the Guild has not adequate capital. The Guild has in a far higher degree what the small builder possessed only in a very low degree and has now ceased to possess at all —ability to produce.

This ability is, of course, dependent on the power of the

Guild to supply, not only the purely manual labour required, but also the necessary technical and administrative ability. If it cannot supply these, it fails as a Guild, and the proposal becomes merely one for the employment by the housing authority of " direct labour " on a collective basis. Even this would be a step in the right direction, and is a step which has been taken by certain Councils, in this country or abroad, both recently and in the past. But the Guild proposal goes much further, and I believe that its advocates are right in thinking that they can carry with them an amply sufficient supply of architectural, technical and managerial ability, the more so as their scheme makes definite provision not merely for the admission of the brain-worker, but for the full recognition of his special competence and function. It proposes to leave the technical man in full control of the technical aspects of the job, and to give him recognition and representation in the counsels of the Guild as a whole.

No one will pretend or imagine that the Guild scheme, however sound it may be, will be absolutely plain sailing, or will not at once find itself faced with big difficulties when it is put into operation. It is not an easy matter to change over all of a sudden from production for profit to production for use under democratic control. But the situation in relation to the housing problem demands a drastic remedy. Hitherto the combined efforts of the Government, the local authorities and the building employers have produced little more than a plentiful output of schemes. The two great difficulties in the way of actual house-building are labour and finance. The financial difficulty is one between the Treasury, the local authorities and the public, which the present scheme does not touch, and which, I believe, only the adoption of a more reasonable attitude in respect both of rents and of financial facilities by the Ministry of Health can overcome. The labour difficulty, which has been growingly recognised as even more serious, the Guild proposal offers a good chance of overcoming ; for it arises not so much from an actual and absolute shortage of labour as from the diversion of the available labour to the wrong type of work—to factory work and luxury building instead of housing schemes. The operatives clearly are in a position to mobilise labour, and this means that, if they can demonstrate, as we think they can, the elementary soundness of their proposal, they will have public opinion overwhelmingly with them. For what the public wants is just houses, and the need for houses comes home to, and profoundly affects, almost every section of the population. If, therefore, a scheme not demonstrably unsound is rejected by the local authorities, the public will most certainly demand to know the reason why. In other words, the nation's need for houses provides the building workers with an unparalleled opportunity to carry the public with them in their demand for the reorganisation of the building industry—or a large part of it—on a real basis of public service.

CHAPTER X

DISTRIBUTION AND THE CO-OPERATIVE MOVEMENT

I

THE DISTRIBUTIVE INDUSTRY

I COME now to the last of the group of industries which I have selected for special treatment in this book. This is the group which centres round Distribution, wholesale and retail, and includes also certain closely allied forms of production. Retail distribution, the point at which the organisation of society on a basis of service comes into direct contact with the domestic consumer, provides the key to the treatment of this problem.

At present, retail trading is organised and carried on by three distinct types of agency. First, and to a very great extent, by small shopkeepers, from the keeper of the tiny village shop to the tobacconist and the second-hand bookseller or curio dealer. Secondly by the big capitalist stores and multiple shops, such as Selfridge's or Harrod's in the first class, and Lipton's or Boots in the second. And, thirdly, by the Co-operative Movement.

The position of the small shopkeeper is similar in several respects to that of the small-scale producer. Either of

them may be merely a worker on his own, employing
nobody outside his own family, or only a single journey-
man or "apprentice." Or he may employ wage-workers,
and thus pass, by unnoticeable stages, into the class of
persons who can be properly termed capitalists. It is as
much an absurdity to call a small tobacconist a capitalist
as it would be to call Mr. Selfridge anything else. A very
large number of shopkeepers occupy, like many small
workshop or factory owners, an intermediate position,
half-way between the "independent producer" and the
capitalist.

About the position of the owners of the big stores or
businesses controlling multiple shops, there is no ambi-
guity. Most of them, like most big capitalist productive
concerns, are limited companies, and they partake to the
full of all the essential characteristics of the capitalist
form of organisation.

The factors which make the problem of distribution
essentially different from that of most of the productive
industries are, first, the presence, in enormous numbers,
of the small shopkeepers; and, secondly, the important
position occupied by the Co-operative Movement. In the
view of the average private trader, the Co-operative Movement is merely a huge multiple shop concern, like Lipton's
or the Maypole, only very much bigger, working in the
market with a great advantage on its side which to the
private trader seems an unfair advantage. In the eyes of
Socialists at least, it must appear very differently; for
this "unfair advantage" is, in fact, nothing less than that
the Co-operative Movement does not work for profit, but
distributes all the commodities in which it deals at cost
price, charging in the first instance, it is true, ordinary
commercial prices, but returning the balance to the cus-

tomer in the form of a dividend on purchases.   The essential fact to realise about the Co-operative Movement is that, except in the insignificant item of "trade with non-members," there is not a ha'p'orth of profit made in it from beginning to end.   It is "distribution for use, and not for profit." [1]

In deciding, therefore, upon the policy which we propose to adopt in dealing with the problem of distribution, it is essential, first of all, to make up our minds about our attitude to the Co-operative Movement.   Apart from this central fact that Co-operation distributes not for profit but for use, and is thereby distinguished clearly and absolutely from all forms of capitalist production, what are the essential points that we have to keep before us in formulating our policy ?   We have to remember that Co-operation is essentially a working-class movement as much as Trade Unionism—a movement created by the workers themselves for the purpose of emancipating themselves from one particular form of capitalist exploitation [2]—a movement directly owned and controlled by a huge section of the working-class.

It would be inconceivably foolish and futile for us either to take up an attitude of opposition to a working-class movement which operates as a distributing agency for use and not for profit, or to allow ourselves, by a failure to seize the possibilities of Co-operation, or to allow fully for it in our vision of the new society, to be forced into an actual opposition to it.   We must recognise the function of Co-operation not only in the society of to-day, but also

[1] Co-operation, in its aspect as a productive agency, is dealt with later in this chapter.   See pp. 200 ff.

[2] The wider theories behind co-operation are also dealt with later. See pp. 197 ff.

in the society of to-morrow : we must seek both to link the two great working-class movements of Trade Unionism and Co-operation firmly together for the fight against Capitalism, and to provide for their harmonious joint action, each within its proper sphere and functions, when Capitalism has been overthrown.

A few years ago, nationalisation and municipalisation were Socialist shibboleths. The nationalisation or municipalisation of *all* the means of production, distribution and exchange was assumed to be essential to the creation of a Socialist Society. To-day, this is no longer the case. Nationalisation and municipalisation are recognised to be useful means to the expropriation of capitalist industries, although even in this sense they are only useful first steps to socialisation ; but the question whether *all* industries must pass through the stage of nationalisation or municipalisation is recognised to be an open question, to be settled, not in accordance with a rigid Collectivist principle, but on lines of expediency involving a consideration of the particular circumstances of each industry or service.

It seems to me to be both wrong and foolish to propose at any stage the nationalisation or municipalisation of the greater part of the distributive services now carried on by the Co-operative Movement. Co-operation is an essentially communal form of organisation, fully as consistent as national or municipal ownership[1] with the working of a Socialist Society. The working-class, which represents the community movement in present-day Society, has developed for itself a particular form of ownership in the large section of the distributive industry which enables

[1] I am not here raising the question of workers' control within the distributive industry, *i.e.* of the Distributive Guild and its relation to Co-operation. To that I shall come shortly.

that section of the industry to be carried on for use and not for profit. This seems to me an excellent *prima facie* reason for not interfering with this form of ownership, but for adopting it as an essential form of community ownership side by side with national and municipal ownership. Moreover, there is another excellent reason why we should accept and welcome Co-operative ownership of industry and the Co-operative form of organisation as essential parts of communial Socialism. The distributive industry, and the forms of production closely allied to it, are distinguished from most of the other industries by the fact that they come into direct contact with the ultimate consumer of individual products. They are not, like the iron and steel, the engineering or the cotton industry, mainly concerned with intermediate products intended for use in subsequent processes of manufacture or service ; they are not, like the public utility services, gas, water, transport, etc., concerned with the supply in bulk of certain continuous services to the whole of the dwellers in a particular area ; they are handling commodities which are mostly bought in small quantities by the individual domestic consumer, in the majority of cases a woman, with a direct exercise of choice and personal fancy.

Accordingly, even if we take it for granted that some form of consumers' representation is necessary and desirable in relation to every industry and service, we may still quite legitimately hold that the forms of representation and organisation should be different in the case of industries and services of widely different types. Forms of representation arising out of national ownership may be desirable in the great productive industries and in national utilities such as coal and railways : forms arising out of municipalisation may suit the bulk services of a more local

13

character ; while for the range of services most closely connected with the individual and domestic consumers Co-operation may well prove to be by far the best form of representation available. Moreover, with the awakening of the public consciousness of women, the Co-operative form of organisation will afford an admirable field for the extension of their influence into the public service, and a means of training for citizenship for the housewife as valuable as Trade Unionism has proved for the industrial workers.

Our consideration, then, of the problem of distribution must begin with a full recognition of Co-operation as the best means of representing the point of view of the working-class consumer. This does not imply any blindness to the shortcomings of the Co-operative Movement, any more than faith in Trade Unionism implies a blindness to the faults of the Trade Unions. What it does imply is the necessity of awakening in the Co-operative Movement the same constructive forces and tendencies as have already been awakened in Trade Unionism, and devoting to the extension of Co-operative membership the same energy as has been devoted to the expansion of Trade Unionism during the last few years.

If a vast expansion of Co-operative distribution is desirable, what is to become of the other forms of distribution which were described at the beginning of this chapter ? For Co-operation to expand so as to drive private traders out of business by direct competition would take, not time, but eternity, even if it were only a question of dealing with the multiple stores and capitalist concerns. As for the small trader, the more he is crushed by competition and driven into the Bankruptcy Court, the more successors seem to arise in his place. We must, then, find some speedier and more effective way than the natural expansion of Co-operation, which is, in any case, seriously checked by the shortage of available capital. As far as the " capitalist " private traders and the big multiple stores are concerned, I suggest nothing less than their expropriation by the State and their transference to the control of the Co-operative Movement. I should like to see the whole working-class movement placing this proposal in the forefront of its programme.

This would not, in itself, deal with the small private shopkeeper, and I do not suggest or desire any such drastic method of dealing with him. The small shopkeeper's continued existence in face of the economic pressure of the big multiple stores is, no doubt, partly the result of his greater willingness, largely enforced by his economic position, for credit transactions ; but it is also and far more the result of the dog's life the shop assistant leads under capitalism, and a natural and healthy expression of his desire for self-government. It may have been very muddle-headed of Kipps to desire to start a shop of his own ; but was he not a better man for the spark of love for freedom which made him do so ? If we could provide for conditions of greater freedom and self-government within the large-scale distributive industry, one of the main incentives to the unnecessary multiplication of small shops would disappear.

I do not mean by this that the small shopkeper would disappear altogether, or that I even wish him to do so. The desire of men of certain types to work " on their own " in preference to forming a part of some larger organisation must be respected, and arises from a deep human instinct which no form of social organisation will remove. If the greater part of the distributive industry were brought under

Co-operative ownership the survival of the small shop-keeper would present no social danger and would be in many respects actually of value. In certain classes of dealing, personal " virtuosity " is every bit as important as a high degree of personal craftsmanship is in certain forms of small-scale production. Just as I believe that the independent craft-master will always survive, and indeed flourish far more than to-day, under a democratic industrial system, so I believe that the small " connoisseur " shop-keeper will survive to a considerable extent. In any case, Heaven forbid that we should herald the coming of economic democracy by assaulting and destroying a class of small service-renderers who are no more capitalists in any real sense that the majority of wage or salary earners! Our job is to overthrow capitalist production by bringing large-scale industry under communal ownership and democratic control. If we can do that, we can well afford to let the loose ends of the economic system adjust themselves in their own way to the new conditions. Let us at all costs avoid becoming narrow doctrinaires and applying our theories in the spirit of the Inquisition.

Our policy, then, should be to let the small shopkeeper alone, and to concentrate, first, on bringing about a really close working alliance between the two great people's movements of Trade Unionism and Co-operation, and on making this alliance no less water-tight in the sphere of theory than in immediate practical politics ; and, secondly, on expanding the number of Co-operators by every means in our power, and demanding and securing the handing over to the Co-operative Movement of the great distributing agencies which are now in the hands of private capitalists

II

CO-OPERATORS AND " NATIONALISERS "

Already, in the joint discussions between Trade Unionists and Co-operators which have become so numerous during the last few years, an apparent cleavage in social policy and ideals has made itself manifest. The Trade Unionists, who have at their Congresses committed themselves to the " nationalisation of the means of production, distribution and exchange," start with a preconception in favour of nationalising or municipalising everything, including ultimately the services now owned and controlled by the Co-operative Movement itself. Co-operators, on the other hand, without anything like so definite a theoretical position, tend to start with a preconception in favour of a gradual extension of Co-operation to all industries and services, although most of them would admit that this will not be practical politics for a very long time to come ; and some would repudiate such idealism altogether, and say that they prefer to avoid " Utopianism," and get on with the practical business of extending Co-operative enterprise when and where they can. While these two points of view remain as at present, without any attempt to find a reconciliation between them, there will always be a grave danger of a practical conflict arising unexpectedly over some particular service or proposal.

Indeed, such a conflict might easily have arisen on two distinct issues during the past two months. Labour has long advocated the municipalisation of the distribution of coal ; but some Co-operative Societies distribute coal to their members, and do it extremely well and at a very low cost. Labour advocates a municipal monopoly in the distribution of milk; but a few Co-operative Societies already distribute milk, and, in some cases at least, do it very much better than the private trader. In the case of coal, the difficulty has been overcome by advocating that it should be open to the local authority to allow a Co-operative Society to act as its agent in distributing coal in its area, and it is almost certain that the same proposal will be adopted in the case of milk. But, sensible as both these compromises are, they do not touch the real difficulty, and they could not be applied to the wider issues of a similar kind which are certain to arise in the near future unless some method of reconciling the divergent points of view is discovered.

What, then, are the essential features of the problem? It has to be considered in two separate aspects, first, in relation to the immediate situation; and, secondly, in relation to the more distant future, and to what is theoretically desirable.

The general principle at which I have hinted already more than once in this chapter is that the Co-operative Movement, extended to cover the whole mass of domestic consumers, is the right organisation for representing the consumers' point of view in relation to those commodities and services which are directly purchased by the individual consumer in small quantities for domestic or personal use, that is, roughly the greater part of the field at present covered by retail trade and certain small allied productive services. On the other hand, it seems to me that a different form of organisation is required for dealing with local public utilities, and another form again for dealing with the great national services and productive industries which do not come into direct contact with the ultimate consumer. I do not say that these three types are necessarily exhaustive in the sense that there are no others ; but they seem to me to cover the three main groups of cases. In the first group, Co-operative ownership affords the solution of the problem, in the second municipal or regional ownership,[1] and in the third national ownership.

This is, of course, only a broad generalisation, which still leaves open many disputes about " border-line " cases. These border-line cases belong to two main types. Either a particular service is in dispute because it is regarded by some as a local " public utility " and by others as a " domestic " service, or a question arises whether a particular form of production is closely enough allied to distribution to be removed from the " nationalisable " into the " co-operative " group.

The cases of the first type are mainly in the sphere of distribution. No one doubts that trams, electricity, gas and water are public utility services, falling definitely within the municipal group. But what about milk distribution ? Milk is essentially, in one aspect, an article of domestic consumption, and therefore seems, when looked at from this point of view, to be plainly " co-operative." But the milk supply is also vitally related to the great municipal and national service of Public Health, and this seems to place it no less clearly in the municipal group. Theoretically, I incline to making milk distribution a co-operative service under Public Health inspection ; but practically this is at present impossible, because there is no chance or hope, under present conditions, of establishing a co-operative monopoly. A monopoly, however, is essential to effective

[1] I am speaking here of municipal ownership without raising the question, discussed in the first chapter of *Self-Government in Industry* (edition of 1919), where there will be several forms of local authority on a functional basis.

supply. There is, therefore, no course left but that which Labour has actually adopted of advocating a municipal monopoly, with power to the local authority to use the Co-operative Society as its agent in distribution.

Or take the case of coal distribution. Coal goes partly to the domestic user, but in much larger quantities it is used by an intermediate consumer for further production or service, as in ships or railways, in the big productive industries like iron and steel manufacture, or in the local utility services such as gas production. In order to secure efficiency and economy, the supply of coal to local factories, utility services and domestic consumers ought to be in the same hands, which can therefore only be those of the local authority, unless, indeed, coal distribution is made a function of the railway service. Here, again, the sensible immediate policy seems to be that of municipal monopoly, with power to use the Co-operative Society as an agent, where this is desired, for retail domestic distribution. The case for Co-operative participation is, however, very much less strong in the case of a bulk service such as coal than in that of milk, and, unless the Co-operative Societies were in some cases already in the field, it would be unnecessary to bring them in.

The reason why some Co-operative idealists will view the above arguments with misgiving is that they fear lest, one by one, under cloak of similar reasonings, all or nearly all the distributive functions of Co-operation may be taken away, and transferred to the local authorities. I certainly do not mean to support any such process. The two cases cited above do seem to me to be exceptional and marginal, and I have no sympathy at all for the municipalising fanatics who want to municipalise everything, including the distributive side of the Co-operative Movement itself.

The second set of marginal cases raises far more difficult problems. On the basis of its distributive activities, both wholesale and retail, the consumers' Co-operative Movement has built up a large number of productive enterprises. Many of the retail stores have their own productive departments, especially in such trades as baking, tailoring, and boot and shoe repairing, and some go further, and own their own farms. The two Co-operative Wholesale Societies have gone much further, and have created, on the basis of their wholesale distributive activities, huge factories manufacturing soap, boots, biscuits, cigarettes, garments, etc., printing works for books and periodicals, flour mills, tea plantations in Ceylon, and other productive enterprises at home and abroad. They engage largely in international trade, and have for this purpose their own fleets of ships. What, they ask, is to happen to all these productive enterprises if the Labour movement pushes to a successful issue its policy of nationalisation of the means of production ? [1]

So far as the great productive industries are concerned, I do not see that Co-operative ownership can be maintained. If the mines are nationalised, the one Co-operative mine will have to be nationalised also. But the mass of the productive operations carried on by the Co-operative Movement is not located in industries to which the policy of nationalisation is likely to be applied soon, and a great many of its operations belong to industries whose nationalisation at any stage seems to me to be extremely doubtful. If the policy advocated in the first part of this chapter

[1] I am here again consciously leaving out of account the question of workers' control in industry, which is dealt with in the next section. Throughout this and the preceding section, the problem is being discussed in terms of ownership.

were carried out and the big multiple stores were transferred by law to the Co-operative Movement, the large productive enterprises of a similar type which they maintain should, I think, be transferred also. I would go further, and say that the right policy to pursue in relation to the whole of such industries as flour-milling, baking, biscuit-making, soap-making, and even such great industries as boot-making and tailoring, is that these should pass by a similar transference under the ownership not of the State or the local authority, but of the Co-operative Movement.

I will go further. One of the most frequent questions addressed to Socialists of any type is, " How would you run the whole business of journalism and publication under Socialism ? " A Guild Socialist can reply, so far as the control is concerned, with a reference to Guild organisation of printers and journalists. But this still leaves unsolved the problem of ownership, and it is widely recognised that a Press owned by the State, or by any central or local government of any kind, would be the very denial of the free Press which we desire. There is no equally strong objection to Co-operative ownership, which would provide both local and national bodies independent of the political machinery of Government and suitable to represent the consumers of printed matter. Books and newspapers are essentially articles of individual or domestic consumption, and therefore fall most naturally into the Co-operative group. I therefore suggest that the printing and publishing industry should be co-operatively owned. A greater localisation of the Press and of authorship generally would, I believe, directly result from free economic conditions, and accordingly the local Co-operative bodies would be more closely concerned than the national bodies with the representation of the consumer of at least daily journalism.

This may sound fantastic to many readers ; but it will only seem so, I think, if they have missed my real point. I am far from suggesting that the Co-operative Movement ought to edit all newspapers and magazines, or that it ought to own all newspapers and magazines. The bulk of journalism under a Guild system would probably consist of either definite organs of some Guild or other social association, or of purely private or group ventures directly supported by their own clientèle. The question I have in mind is that of the ownership of big printing-presses and of the business side of daily newspapers. I do not suggest a Co-operative monopoly of the ownership of all printing plants ; but I do suggest that the larger plants, both for newspaper and book production and for general printing, should be owned co-operatively rather than by a local or national authority. The co-operatively-owned and Guild-controlled printing works would then take their orders, without drawing political or other partisan distinctions, from Guilds, other associations, voluntary groups or individuals. Co-operative ownership is to be preferred, because it would afford better safeguards than any other form of " public " ownership for a free Press responsive to the demands of groups and individuals of every kind. At the same time, there is no reason why small-scale private presses should not continue and even develop to a far greater extent than they can to-day.

This is not to suggest that a great productive and " service " industry such as printing and publishing should be regarded as a branch of, or subordinated to, distribution, but that the mission of Co-operation concerns a much wider range of activities than distribution alone, and that the distributive service will, indeed, be only one of a number falling within the co-operatively owned, as distinguished from the nationally owned or the municipally owned, group.　Certain small-scale forms of production, such as boot-repairing and some kinds of dressmaking, will probably be directly connected, in the future as they are now, with the distributive service ; but in addition to, and quite apart from, these, there will be whole industries and services under Co-operative ownership and related to the Co-operative Movement in the same way as other industries and services will be related to local or national public authorities.　The next section, which deals with the productive, or Guild, organisation of these industries, should serve to make my meaning perfectly clear.

I believe that a recognition of this division of industries and services into these various types, in which national, municipal or Co-operative ownership should be aimed at according to the character of each industry or service, would afford a basis on which a really stable alliance between Trade Unionism and Co-operation could be built up. This alliance would, of course, have to include also an agreement on the questions of control, as distinct from ownership, dealt with in the next section.　If an agreement could be come to on these two points, the whole working-class movement would gain an enormous accession of strength in its day to day struggle against exploitation ; for a common ultimate social programme would make possible, what is hardly possible to-day, a real working alliance between the two movements in present-day economic and political action.

III

Co-operation and Workers' Control

The Co-operative Movement, apart from the small number of societies of producers in such industries as boot-making, textiles and a few others, is a movement of *consumers*. The form of industrial control which it represents is consumers' control, and the position of the worker employed by a Co-operative Society is, from the standpoint of control, no more satisfactory than the position of a worker in private, or in State, employment. In a wider sense, it is better than that of the employee of a private business, because the Co-operative Society produces and distributes for use and not for profit ; but this only places the Co-operative employee in the same position as the employee of the State or of a local authority. There is, however, one further important difference which, while it has so far produced little or no practical effect, is strong reason for hope. The employers of the Co-operative employee, that is, the Co-operative members, are predominantly working-class and largely Trade Unionist. They can, therefore, hardly be unaffected by the strong movement among the Trade Unionists for democratic control of industry, and, if a practical programme of democratic control in the Co-operative Movement can be placed clearly before them, they can be brought to support it and to overcome any opposition which the bureaucracy of Co-operation may offer.

If Guild Socialist arguments are sound at all, then the Co-operative Movement, as an organisation of consumers, is no more fitted to *manage* industry thant he State or a local authority. The arguments in favour of control by the workers actually engaged in the service hold good just as much of the distributive and other services in which the Co-operative Movement is engaged as of other industries and services, and the position is, *in this respect*, in no way affected by the fact that Co-operation is a working-class movement producing for use and not for profit. This last fact, however, while it does not affect the need for producers' control, does profoundly affect the methods to be adopted in securing it.

Let us compare the position of the employees of the Co-operative Movement in demanding control, first, with the position of workers under a private capitalist employer, and secondly, with that of workers under the State or a local authority. In the first case, the difference is obvious. Since Co-operation is a working-class movement not producing for profit and well fitted to express the point of view of the domestic consumer, there is clearly no need to change the ownership of the service, so far as it is concerned with domestic utilities, and no such objection to " joint control " as exists in the case of private capitalism. Indeed, whereas the difference of motive makes " joint control " impossible in a capitalist industry except on the basis of a surrender by the workers to capitalist ideas, there is no such difficulty in the way of joint control between Trade Unionists and Co-operators. This does not mean that, in the case of Co-operative employees, joint control is a substitute for encroaching control, but that it is available as an additional method which enables workers' control to be pushed further than it can be under a private employer.

The position of the Co-operative employee is much more like that of the employee of a public authority, and, given the requisite demand among the Co-operative employees themselves, is at least as favourable to the winning of control as that of the employees of a public authority actually dominated by Labour. It is distinctly more favourable than that of a State employee, and will remain so as long as nationalised industries are owned by a State dominated by capitalist ideas and motives. " Joint control " is, to some extent, possible for State employees, because direct production for profit is eliminated from nationalised services ; but it is much easier for Co-operative employees, because it means joint control with a movement dominated by their own class.

This being so, there are clearly, in the process of winning control in the services owned by the Co-operative Movement, two sides to be considered. There is, first, the question of the steps to be taken by Co-operative employees themselves ; and secondly, there is the question of the way in which Co-operators should meet the demands which their employees put forward.

In distribution, with which we are mainly concerned, no less than in productive industries, any real " control " movement must begin mainly at the bottom. The shop or store is to distribution what the workshop is to industry, and has the advantage of being at least as favourable a field as the workshop for the assumption by the workers of a substantial measure of control. The Shop Steward and the Shop Committee have as important a part to play in the distributive industries as their namesakes have in engineering. The first step towards any real control movement is the general formation of Shop Committees and Store Committees based on an effective Shop Stewards' movement throughout the distributive industry—for this first step, unlike some of the subsequent steps, is just as well suited to the capitalist multiple shop businesses as to the Co-operative Stores.

These Shop and Store Committees, like the Shop and Works Committees in productive industries, should aim at a steady transference into their hands of as much of the control of the shop and store as they can conveniently assimilate.   They should adopt the measures described in a previous chapter under the name of " Collective Contract," [1] insist on control over engagements and dismissals, over methods of payment, over the appointment of departmental and branch managers, over the detailed organisation of work in the shop or department, substituting, wherever possible, for the individual relation of each employee to the " management," a collective relation of all the workers.   These steps, again, apply equally to Co-operative and to capitalist distributive enterprise.

But, whereas in a capitalist concern not one of these steps is likely to be successfully taken without a struggle, in Co-operative employment, if the situation is rightly handled, it may be possible not only to take these steps, but to go considerably further, with the assent and goodwill, if not always of the bureaucrats of Co-operation, at any rate of the mass of the members of the Co-operative Societies.   Thus, I believe that Co-operative employees, when they have set up their departmental and Store Committees of Shop Stewards, can safely and usefully take at once a further step, and demand in each department, and for the Store as a whole, joint committees equally representing the employees and the elected Committee of the Co-operative Society.   This joint body would be, not a substitute for the assumption of shop control by the workers themselves, but a body which

[1] See pp. 154 ff.

would, rightly used, greatly facilitate the transference
and provide for a close contact, at every stage of the
process, with the elected representatives of the consumers.
This double process of encroaching control and joint
control might result in the gradual transformation, without
a sharp break at any point, of the Trade Union of Co-
operative employees into a Guild, and of the Co-operative
Movement into a consumers' organisation no longer
directly controlling industry, but representing as owner
the standpoint of the consumers in relation to the
Guild.

Of course, I do not assume that this process will be
absolutely smooth and effortless. Co-operative employees
must be prepared to fight, and will have, on occasion, to
fight, for control against a recalcitrant Co-operative Society
dominated by a bureaucracy hostile to the new ideas.
But, on the whole, if they appeal directly to the Co-operative members, who are themselves largely Trade Unionists,
I believe that they can secure the election of committees
which will really represent the consumer and take a view
in which the aspirations of men as consumers and producers will be reconciled. Workers' control in distribution, as well as in other industries, is in the interest of
consumers at least as much as of producers. The whole
argument that the consumer will be best served if he leaves
the organisation of service in the hands of the service-
renderers, applies to the services controlled by Co-operation
as much as elsewhere. It is not because I want the Co-
operator Trade Unionist to take the producer's rather than
the consumer's point of view that I suggest an appeal to
him, if necessary, over the head of his committee. It is
because I believe that the Guild solution offers the best
reconciliation and expression of both points of view that I

14

think an appeal based upon it is likely to persuade the
rank and file Trade Unionist Co-operator.

But, it will be asked, if the Co-operative Committee is
no longer to manage the Store, what will its functions be ?
Will it not become useless and disappear ? By no means.
The Committee does not in reality manage the Store to-
day : it leaves that to the manager. Its function, which
would remain to it and be far better exercised if it were
relieved of its supposed function of management, would be
that of representing the point of view, and making effective
the demand, of the consumers. It would fulfil this function
by constant consultation with the workers entrusted with
the management of the Store, by criticism of them, and in
dealing with such matters as the fixing of prices or taking
up a complaint with other Guilds from which the Distributive Guild would draw its supplies. Moreover, as we
saw in an earlier section of this chapter, the Co-operative
body would remain the actual owner of the means of distribution and of the means of production closely allied to
distribution. It would thus have a direct responsibility
in connection with all questions of capital outlay, building
and development of Stores and branches, and all other
general financial questions relating to the service of distribution. These functions alone would certainly suffice to
keep the Co-operative Committees busy on important work
under the new conditions. In addition, I believe they would
have an important position as a recognised and integral
part of the structure of local government ; but a consideration of this point would take us too far afield from our
present purpose.

The conclusions, then, at which we have arrived are,
first, that the principles of workers' control are no less
applicable to services owned by the Co-operative Move-

ment than to those under other forms of public ownership; secondly, that a greatly enlarged sphere of activity will remain to co-operatively-owned enterprise even when national and municipal ownership have achieved their full development ; and, thirdly, that to a great extent it should prove possible to make the transition to Guild control in the Co-operative Movement by agreement instead of force, if Trade Unionists and Co-operators can be persuaded to reach a common understanding about their ideals and objects as a basis for a common policy in dealing with immediate questions.

CHAPTER XI

THE FINANCE OF INDUSTRY

I

SPECULATION AND THE WORKER

ALMOST every week during 1919 brought fresh news of gigantic deals, running into many millions, in the shares of various industrial concerns and companies. The Lancashire cotton industry, which had been somewhat remarkably free from the operation of big financial interests whose concern is purely speculative, is the latest victim. For months past, one Lancashire cotton mill after another has been changing hands at a valuation artificially inflated by speculation, and most of these transactions have been accompanied by the formation of new companies, whose share capital is based upon the inflated value at which the property has been acquired. In fact, the " outside " financier and the Lancashire mill-owner are at present congenially engaged in capitalising and sharing the " prosperity " resulting from the war.

Under present conditions, this process is, no doubt, in some degree inevitable ; for the actual material value of the plant in a cotton mill, as in every other industrial establishment, has greatly increased owing to the heavy cost of building and equipping any new factory at the present time.   This, however, is not the only cause of the present boom in speculation or of the incursion of financiers into the industry.   Another cause is to be found in the high profits prevailing and expected in the industry even when the increased cost of buildings and plant is taken fully into account.   And a third cause is direct inflation of values in a narrower sense—the acquisition of properties at a high value by financiers who intend not to produce cotton goods, but to resell at the first opportunity at an even higher price than they have paid.

The first of these phenomena is one which is common, not only to all manufacturing industry, but to almost all forms of material property.   The boom in house property, especially in property above the Rents Restriction Acts level, shows exactly the same process at work. The net effect clearly is to make a vast present in unearned increment to all owners of such property.   Quite apart from the deliberate creation of secret reserves by firms and companies, the increase in prices and in cost of production has been automatically creating huge reserves which are now beginning to be capitalised either by such transactions as those which are taking place in the cotton industry and elsewhere, or by the issue of huge blocks of bonus shares to existing shareholders, or by the offer of facilities to existing shareholders to acquire new shares at prices far below their market value.

All the processes described above have the most serious consequences both for the workers employed in the industries affected and for that part of the public which does not share to any real extent in the new wealth that is being created.   From the workers' point of view the effects are obviously disastrous.   A cotton mill, let us say, changes hands at a price six times as great as the pre-war market value of its capital. This transaction is followed by the flotation of a new company with a capital based on this new value, and very likely with an admixture of "water" over and above the price actually paid. At once a new expectation of profit is created. In order to pay 6 per cent under the new conditions, the mill has now to make a profit equivalent to 36 per cent under the old. The new shareholders, having bought their shares at the new value, will certainly not regard themselves as profiteers if they claim this 6 per cent as reasonable dividend. Six per cent will look to the public a quite moderate figure, and the facts that a huge unearned increment of capital has passed into the hands of the old shareholders, and that the financiers who carried through the transaction have levied a further toll upon the proceeds of the cotton industry, if they are ever generally noticed, will speedily be covered up and forgotten. Exactly the same situation is created by the issue of free bonus shares or of new shares at less than their present value to existing shareholders. A huge new claim upon the industry by the owning classes will have been established, and, while the new rates of dividend will appear to the general public to be modest and inoffensive, it will be none the less true that the expectation of profit from the labours of a given number of workers operating a given plant will have been greatly augmented.

This will be a serious matter for the workers directly concerned when they come to ask for a concession in wages, hours or conditions of labour. They will be met with the reply that "the industry cannot bear" the concession, and the estimate of what the industry can bear will always be based upon the new capital values and the new expectation of profit. Moreover, if the workers retort that they refuse to recognise this new standard, they will be politely informed that most of the existing shareholders have acquired their holdings at the new values, and that it is accordingly unreasonable to hold them responsible. If the workers go on to inquire what has become of the old shareholders who have absorbed the difference between the new value and the old, it will be impossible to trace them ; for many of them will have departed with their unearned increment to seek fields for investment elsewhere. The erection of new capital values therefore presents an effectual barrier to the workers when they seek to raise wages and improve conditions at the expense of excessive profits.

The public, in its capacity as consumer, is also directly affected ; for the heightened expectation of profit also affects the level of prices, and does so most of all when the new conditions include the reduction or elimination of competition by the creation of price-fixing rings, cartels to regulate production, or actual trusts. In this connection, again, the dividing of shares and the creation of new companies with a share capital based on the new values afford protection against any attempt by the community to regulate prices by the limitation of profits; for limitation to a given percentage on the present share values allows the whole of the excess to escape, while limitation in terms of pre-war values is very difficult in face of the change of ownership.

Society has, then, no ready means of dealing with the situation created by the incursion of high finance into the sphere of any particular industry, except in those cases in which the industry is already State controlled and can be transferred to public ownership on the basis of pre-war values. Where, as in the cotton industry, real control has never been in operation, or where, as in shipping and engineering, it has been hastily removed on the termination of hostilities, there is literally no way, within the industry itself, of handling the situation, or of relieving the pressure upon the workers and the public caused by the inflation of values and the swollen expectation of profit. The capture of the proceeds by the investing classes can, indeed, be mitigated by heavier and more steeply graduated taxation, and a proportion of the new *rentier* claim on industry can be liquidated by the method of the capital levy; but in so far as these are regarded wholly as methods of paying interest on and paying off the war debt, the new expectation of profit from any particular industry is not affected. The workers are still faced by this obstacle in their demand for better conditions ; the consumer is still faced by it in his demand for lower prices.

How greatly this affects the workers in such an industry as the cotton industry may not be readily appreciated by those who think of industry mainly in terms of those sections of it which are most talked of in the Press. Wages and conditions in the cotton trade have always been determined largely by considerations of what the industry will bear, or, in other words, have been less a basic charge than a residuary factor in cost of production. In face of the changed conditions, it is impossible that the cotton operatives, or other groups of operatives who are similarly circumstanced, should continue to accept this position, or to admit that the new expectation of profit is to be satisfied before they become entitled to an improved standard of life. The record of the cotton industry as the chosen home of industrial peace is likely to be rudely broken. Already the widespread speculation and the increasing concentration of capital in the industry are producing a marked effect upon the mentality of the workers. A new spirit is abroad, and future demands will be far more extensive, and far more aggressively pushed, than has been the case in the past. A few years ago no one would have regarded the nationalisation of the cotton industry as practical politics in any immediate sense ; but to-day nationalisation as a remedy for the present situation is being seriously discussed in every Lancashire town. Nationalisation, however, at present values would be, from a financial point of view, largely a case of locking the door when the steed has been stolen.

The cotton industry has been taken as a leading example of a general tendency—the readjustment of capitalist values to the changed level of prices, and the absorption by the investing classes of the unearned increment of war. This is as important a part of the " vicious circle " as the relation declared to exist between prices and wages, and it is a phenomenon far more serious in its effects for all those classes which depend upon fixed incomes, whether in the form of salaries or of fixed interest as opposed to varying profits. At present we are helplessly watching this process of adjustment at work, and the circle of capitalistic ideas affords absolutely no means of dealing with it. It is, indeed, on the capitalistic hypothesis, not merely justifiable but inevitable. Nevertheless, it is not likely to be popular if its meaning is clearly understood ; for it amounts, in effect, to the placing of war profits and war expectations of profit upon a permanent and socially recognised basis, with a view to sanctifying for the next generation a distribution of property and income even worse than that which was found so galling by the last. Almost every day a new company is floated to make one million pounds of pre-war capital into several, or the same object is even more simply achieved by the issue of bonus shares. Every one of these transactions sets the seal of social recognition upon a new and lively expectation of profits to come, and thereby fastens the shackles of profiteering industry more firmly upon the wage-earners and the public. And every day that this process continues makes the recognition more complete, until the new claim passes smoothly from a claim *nisi* into a claim absolute. All this, in face of the increasing revolt of Labour against the old conditions in industry, draws us nearer to the rapids of revolution and farther from the green and pleasant land of "Reconstruction" which we have been told to expect. The hand of finance lies heavy on industry and on the public; and until that hand is removed the standard of life of the worker by hand and brain will be menaced and an effective obstacle will be interposed in the way of any substantial fall in the cost of living.

II

A Wasting Asset

When the owner of an industrial plant, for the purposes of some commercial transaction, reckons up his assets, he takes account of buildings, plant, stock, reserves, holdings in other concerns, and all the various forms of fixed and floating capital in his possession. But there is one factor which, though it is no less essential to production than buildings, plant and material, never appears in an industrial balance-sheet. That factor is the co-operation of Labour— or, in other words, the willingness of the workers employed in the concern to produce wealth in return for a standard wage, and the observance of certain minimum conditions of employment laid down by their Trade Unions. This invisible asset, which appears in no balance-sheet, is nevertheless just as essential to the continuance of production under the economic system of capitalism as all the material and other assets which pass under the name of " capital." Indeed, capital itself, as distinguished from land and natural resources, is the result of the past co-operation of Labour in production.

In the past, the willingness of Labour to place its services at the disposal of the plant-owner in return for a wage has been the assumption on which not only production itself, but every credit transaction which stands behind production, has been conducted. When a manufacturer raises a loan, the lender lends to him not so much because he owns so much capital as because he believes him to have the power to secure the production of commodities of such and such a value, and believes that these commodities will be the borrower's to dispose of when they have been produced. In other words, credit transactions in relation to industry tacitly imply that the borrower, that is, in this case the employer, has control over labour and is in a position to induce the labourer to work for him. It is true that employers themselves, by introducing special " strike clauses " into their contracts, have of late years betrayed to their customers the fact that their control over labour is becoming less absolute; but the strike has at most only been regarded as an abnormal and temporary interruption of the normal working of industry, and not as an alteration in the basis of industry itself.

The position in this respect is changing, although the full effects of the change are as yet hardly being felt in this country. At present the change can best be illustrated by its effects on the international market. There are already more than a few countries on the continent of Europe to whose capitalists a British financier or exporter would think twice before giving any substantial credit, not so much because the countries in question are impoverished as because the control of their capitalists over the workers and the willingness of their workers to go on producing under the old system can no longer safely be taken for granted. Russia was a case in point, even before the Bolshevik revolution, and Central Europe and the new States which have arisen as a result of the war furnish other examples. Every person interested in finance and credit operations knows well that an access of labour unrest is a sound commercial reason, if not for withholding credits, at any rate for raising the rate of interest demanded, and so insuring against possible loss.

This statement holds good not only of international economic operations but also of industry at home. The credit of British manufacturers is based not on their " capital," but upon the assurance of their future possession of marketable commodities which results from their control of both plant and labour. If they cease, and in proportion as they cease, to control either of these factors in production, their credit goes, and commercial operations become impossible because the assurance of capitalist production disappears.

It is beyond doubt that the employer in this country, like employers in other countries, is losing his control over Labour. This does not mean that the workers in all industries are dramatically refusing to produce, or demanding with one voice the immediate establishment of the Co - operative Commonwealth. But it does mean that their dissatisfaction—or the dissatisfaction of an effective proportion among them—with capitalist production is reaching a point at which it seriously intereferes with the further conduct of industry along the traditional lines.

Two instances from the Labour side and one from the financial side will serve to illustrate clearly what I mean. The present situation in the mining industry is the direct result of an ultimatum presented by the miners withdrawing their previous co-operation with the mine-owners in the production of coal. This is made perfectly clear by their refusal to enter the "Duckham" scheme proposed by the Government as a substitute for nationalisation. A situation has thus been created which is unprecedented in the industry of this country. The case for and against mines' nationalisation is being argued and thought about, not primarily as a commercial problem in the ordinary sense, but as a fundamental question of human relationships and of social system. The nationalisation of mines is inevitable, if only because the labour asset of the mining industry will be withdrawn from effective co-operation under any other conditions.

I do not mean that, if the Government persisted in its refusal to nationalise the mines and were still able to maintain itself in office despite its refusal, the miners would, or could, remain for ever on strike. They might, I have no doubt, even be defeated if they struck and were forced to go back to the pits. But they could not be forced to work hard or well. In fact, the asset of their co-operation in industry would in that case not disappear completely or suddenly, but it would be a steadily wasting asset in proportion to the diminishing energy which would be put into production.

This, in its turn, would affect the whole economic operation of the industry. It would mean a heavier overhead cost, and therefore a larger demand for capital, in respect of every ton of coal produced ; and unless the industry were fully subsidised in some way, it would mean increased difficulty in attracting fresh capital and in developing new sources of production. At present the uncertainty of the mining position is largely preventing the mine-owners from being willing to invest fresh capital in the industry, or even to make good depreciation out of reserves. If it were not for the practical certainty that, in the last resort, the State will come to the aid of the mine-owners and buy them out on unduly favourable terms, the present attitude of the miners would make it almost impossible to secure new capital, and would have already caused a dramatic slump in the market value of mining shares, in spite of the very high profits which prevail at present.

Our second instance can be drawn from almost any industry in which the workers are strongly organised. Dislike of the present economic system is in almost all industries already responsible for a fall in average output and in intensity of work. Indeed, the vast propaganda which is being conducted by employers in favour of " increased production " is at least as much an attempt to counteract the forces which are making for decreased production as an endeavour to "speed up" the workers on American lines of mass-production. It is the product of fear more than of any other motive.

Our third instance shall be financial. Broadly speaking, the rate of interest which the lender or investor expects varies with the security that the money will be paid regularly, year in and year out. Gilt-edged securities carry a low rate of interest ; the speculative investor looks for a high rate to cover his risk. One reason at least for " profiteering " and for the increasing prevalence of abnormally high profits is that all industries are in process of becoming "speculative." The investor wants a high profit, partly at least because "he knoweth not when his hour cometh." The sensitive barometer of finance is already registering the pressure of industrial democracy.

With this wasting of the assets of capitalism goes necessarily, for the general public, a decrease in efficiency of service. This decrease finds expression in high prices, in defective quality, and in actual failure of supply. This, in turn, aggravates the unrest which is one of its causes. The real and ultimate vicious circle of to-day is not the circle of wages and prices, but the circle of unrest and under-production. From this circle there is no way out merely by waiting for something to turn up; for, although something will undoubtedly turn up, it is quite certain, as long as this policy is pursued, to be something bad, at least for the general public and for Society as a whole. A radical, if gradual, change of industrial system is essential ; and this change must include a restoration of the co-operation of Labour in production on a new basis.

The old co-operation of labour was, in fact, really not co-operation but subordination. Although the product was only produced by the coming together of capital (in the forms of natural resources and products of past labour) and of present labour, the whole "credit" went to the employer on the strength of his possession of capital and of his control, amounting almost to possession, of labour. The increased strength and organisation, and still more the growing education and consciousness, of the workers have made the maintenance of the old relation impossible. Profit-sharing proposals, futile as they are, amount to a tardy and inadequate attempt to recognise labour-power itself as a form of capital entitled to a "dividend," as one employer recently expressed it in a co-partnership proposal.

But the desire of the workers is not to have their "labour-power" assimilated to capital, or to become partners in production for profit. They are withdrawing their co-operation not only because they feel the unfairness of their present subordination, but because an increasing number of them are visualising the possibility of an organisation of production directed to use, and not to profit. This may be regarded as a worn phrase, but it is more and more coming to represent a very lively and actual sentiment.

This means nothing less than that the financial system of capitalism is tottering to its fall. The collapse may not be dramatic or sudden, but it is certain. Production on a large scale for profit can only be conducted on a "credit" basis. The willingness of the lender to grant credit depends on his confidence in the borrower's ability, not to produce, but to get possession of products. The capitalist's ability to do this depends on his retaining control both of plant and of labour. His control of labour is already impaired, and the credit basis of industry is already suffering a corresponding damage. If Labour's co-operation is further withdrawn, capitalist credit will be further impaired. If credit dwindles, the possibility of capitalist production dwindles with it. A process is already at work of which the necessary culmination, unless it can be arrested by a counter-movement, is the collapse of capitalist production.

III

NEXT STEPS

The increase of speculation and the disturbance by labour unrest of the credit basis of industry are two aspects of a single process. Naturally, such a situation has called into activity a number of attempts to redress the balance. The most obvious of these is the attempt to recapture Labour support for capitalist production by the offering of special incentives to increase output, and by attempting to entangle the workers with capitalist production through such devices as profit-sharing and co-partnership which are now reviving in many new and "liberalised" forms as a direct result of the increased strength of Labour, and of its growing opposition to the whole structure of capitalist industry.

It is not necessary to waste much breath in demonstrating the futility of this campaign. Appeals to the workers to increase their output will succeed only when they can be convinced that they are producing for use and not for profit, and therefore producing necessaries rather than luxuries, and satisfying the needs of the many rather than the appetitiveness of the few. Financial incentives may have a temporary success in certain cases ; but he who speeds up to-day in order to earn more will speed down to-morrow in the process of bargaining over piece-rates or bonus times. No piece-work or efficiency system has yet been devised which will permanently make men work hard if they see no moral reason why they should. And, under capitalism, there is no moral reason.

Nor does a better fate await the proposals for new forms of profit-sharing and co-partnership, even when these are purged of the features which made so many of the older schemes fundamentally inconsistent with Trade Union principles. In isolated factories, no doubt, profit-sharing schemes will be adopted with results which capitalists will regard as beneficial ; but the effect of these schemes too will speedily wear off, and Capital and Labour, working with fundamentally inconsistent motives, will find them-

15

selves face to face as before. Moreover, there is little
or no chance that profit-sharing or co-partnership will be
adopted except in isolated cases ; and its adoption in a
few cases will have absolutely no effect upon the general
development of the industrial situation, which will depend
mainly on the position in the big vital industries, where
profit-sharing and co-partnership are least capable of being
applied with success. The plain fact is that real joint
control of industry by capitalists and workers is impossible,
because control, in order to be even passably efficient,
must be in the hands of a homogeneous body animated by
a common purpose.

The capitalist remedies for the withdrawal of Labour
co-operation being futile, sundry new ideas for a peaceful
transition from capitalistic credit to a better and more
stable system are being mooted. The *New Age* has for
some time been combining with a relentless and conclusive
exposure of the capitalist credit system a number of
barely intelligible hints of a solution which its writers suppose themselves to have discovered. I do not believe that
anyone could make out, from the references so far published, exactly what this solution is ; and I do not pretend
to have achieved the impossible. It is, however, clear
that the proposal somehow centres round the creation
of workers' banks, which are to finance industry, using as
the basis of their credit the labour-power of the workers.
Whether or not this is exactly the substance of the *New
Age* proposal, it is at least a proposal which is circulating
to a considerable extent at the present time. It is therefore necessary to inquire whether there is " anything
in it."

Clearly, if the workers can make their unexhausted
labour-power a basis of credit, they can themselves col-

lectively or individually become capitalists or *entrepreneurs*
by financing industry on credit and absorbing by this
means a growing proportion of the future surplus. But
can they ? As we saw in the first section, the credit of
the capitalist has been based, not merely on his control of
" plant," but on his prospective possession of the product,
which involves the control, not only of " plant," but also
of " labour-power." In exactly the same way, Labour,
under the conditions of the credit system, could only
make its " labour-power " a basis of credit if it had some
assurance of a prospective possession of the product.
In order to have this, it would need to combine with the
control of " labour-power " the control of " plant," or,
in other words, to have already possessed itself of the
natural resources and products of expended " labour-power "
which are required for further production. Thus, it would
only be possible for the workers to find in their " labour-
power " a basis for credit independent of capital if the
great change, which some persons hope to accomplish with
the aid of this new form of credit, had already been accomplished by other means. So far, then, we seem to be
entitled to dismiss this proposed solution, and to cry
" As you were."

This, however, is not a complete answer to the suggestion. For, while it would be impossible for the workers to
erect their monopoly of labour-power into an adequate
basis for credit independently of the capitalist, it is quite
an agreeable proposition that, by securing the control of
their own labour-power and denying its use to the capitalists
except upon terms, the workers might claim a share in
credit, and compel the capitalists to accept their claim.
If what we have said above is true, then, with the withdrawal of Labour's subordination, the basis of capitalist

credit is destroyed; for the two factors, whose unity in a single hand is essential to credit, are now divided, and one is in the hands of each antagonist. This being so, one of two things must happen. Either the present credit basis of industry must go, and be replaced by a system of national and other public ownership and finance, such as we have proposed in the foregoing chapters, or Capital and Labour must agree and unite their forces on a new basis for the re-establishment of credit. But it should be clearly understood that, while a joint command of credit by capitalists and workers, based on their respective controls of "plant" and "labour-power," is in itself perfectly possible, credit, under such an arrangement, could only be raised by the two parties acting jointly, and not by either acting in isolation from the other. The practicability, therefore, of such a rebuilding of the credit basis of industry depends upon a wider question, already discussed in earlier chapters of this book—on the possibility of any stable reconciliation and alliance between the now opposed forces of Capital and Labour. If I am right in maintaining that, on any general basis at least, such a reconciliation or alliance is altogether out of the question, I cannot be wrong in holding that there is "nothing in" the proposal to find a way out of capitalism by using the "labour-power" of the workers as a basis for credit, and so hoisting the capitalist engineer with his own petard.

The essential condition of a constructive escape from capitalist finance, and the only means of averting the impending collapse of industry, is to transfer the means of production, as rapidly as possible, from private ownership to some form of public ownership, whether national, municipal, Co-operative or something differing from all these but harmonious with them. Of course, if the method

of transference is that of purchase, which, short of a real
social revolution, may be regarded as inevitable, none of
these methods will directly result in the dispossession of
the present owners of their claim to a share in the national
product. It will, by itself, only convert them from
profiteers or private-interest-takers to *rentiers* of the
State or some other public or quasi-public body. But
from such a change three advantages result. By far the
least of these is that, if the price paid is not an inflated
price, future increments are secured for the community.
A second advantage is that the way is made clear for an
appeal to a new motive in industry, and for the development of effective industrial democracy. The third advantage is that, in becoming a pure *rentier*, the capitalist,
qua capitalist, becomes an obviously functionless person,
claiming a share in the national product in return for
absolutely no service rendered to the community. His
dispossession by the community is thus rendered completely certain, and can take place without even the
smallest disturbance of the industrial system. The
logical outcome of public purchase is expropriation :
nationalisation, and other similar immediate steps, are
half-way houses to socialisation. This being so, it does
not even very much matter if, in purchasing, the community pays an inflated price.

But, I suppose, it is still necessary, even after half a
century of Socialist propaganda, to say why socialisation
is not " killing the goose that lays the golden eggs," or
rather to state positively how fresh capital would be
provided under a new industrial system based on production for use instead of profit. Fresh capital for industry,
under present conditions, is supplied partly by individuals by the process somewhat misleadingly described as

" saving," and partly by firms by the retention in the business of sums which might otherwise be distributed as profits. In either case, the result is that in any year only part of the labour-power expended is used for the production or distribution of commodities for immediate consumption, while another part is devoted to maintaining and improving the means of production. At present, the balance between " saving " and " spending " is not preserved by any communal action, but is left to the unchecked operation of private motives. A company may starve its reserve funds in order to make a large distribution of profits, or it may build up large open or secret reserves and content itself with a smaller distribution : an individual may "live up to his income," or he may live on considerably less than his income, and invest the balance in the hope of increasing his wealth. New capital at present is subscribed mostly, although not entirely, by those richer sections of society known, in this connection, as " the investing classes " ; but, by whosoever it may be subscribed, it comes out of the product of industry.

If, then, the means of production were communally owned, and there were no investing classes—if there were no "inducement to save " and no " individual thrift "— this would not mean that new capital could not be supplied to industry, but that the community as a whole would have to take in hand the decision as to the balance of "saving" and " spending" which it now leaves to the blind play of economic forces. Every industry, operating as a democratic public concern, would have to make provision in its annual budget for the replacement of its capital in face of amortisation, and the community itself would have to decide to what industries and services, and in what measure, new capital should be supplied, and to take the necessary steps to ensure a balance between ultimate consumption of the product of each industry, and the creation of fresh publicly owned capital, to be raised by direct taxation of the industries themselves. Such a communal assumption of responsibility for saving would make it possible for the first time both to ensure that the general balance should correspond to the best estimates of human needs, and to see that production was diverted into those channels in which it was most required, and not into those through which the capitalist might expect to secure the maximum amount of profit.

The way, then, out of the morass of capitalist finance lies not through any " fancy " schemes of " labour credit " or the like, but through the assumption of collective control by the community of its own financial affairs. An essential part of this process is the national ownership of the service of banking—not its splitting-up on industrial lines.   We should socialise our banking service, and so establish a communal control over the issue of credit even while private capitalism remains.   In so doing, we should be striking a shrewd blow at the whole structure of capitalist industrialism ;   for behind the capitalist manufacturer is always the money power of the banks and financial houses.   As we succeed in establishing democratic self-government in the various industries and services, it will be necessary to admit the democratic organisations controlling them to a share in the control of the banking system.   In a Guild Society, while the internal management and control of the banks would, of course, be placed in the hands of those actually engaged in the service of banking, the external control of policy would have to be vested in some body effectively representing the several points of view of the various sections of producers and consumers. Banking is a key service, and ought least of all to be left in the hands of any private or sectional interest.

The socialisation of banking would ensure a certain measure of collective control over speculation. But this national control would, of course, while the State continues to be controlled by capitalists, be exercised largely in the interests of capitalism itself. Speculation is, in some measure, inherent in capitalism, and is even bound to become worse as the capitalist "asset" of Labour subordination continues to waste. There is no escape from its consequences, evil as we have seen them to be, short of the overthrow of capitalism itself, and its replacement by a communal system of industry and finance. The extension of public ownership and democratic control over both industry and banking, while it will not get rid of the financial embarrassment of capitalism, will pave the way to the further, and really vital, step of destroying capitalism altogether, and will make it possible to take this step without any serious disturbance of the productive forces of society. It is therefore the right policy to pursue in the immediate future, and I hope especially that any future Labour Government will make one of its earliest measures the socialisation of the whole system of banking and " high " finance.

CHAPTER XII

THE REAL CLASS STRUGGLE

IN the orthodox presentation of the theory of the class struggle, the "proletariat," or the working-class, is depicted as struggling to throw off the tyranny of the "bourgeoisie," or of the capitalist class. Society is regarded as divided into two hostile classes, between which the struggle must continue as long as they continue to exist as classes. This is no doubt recognised as a simplification of the facts of any existing society ; but it is put forward as being essentially and fundamentally true as an analysis of the economic conditions which exist under the present industrial system.

If I am John Jones, general labourer, I shall probably find little difficulty in recognising to which of these contending classes I belong, in the event of my ever putting the question to myself at all. If I am Sir John Jones, M.P., financier and director of many companies, I shall hardly find greater difficulty, in the event of my demeaning myself to read the literature in which such low matters are discussed. But, if I am John Jones, M.D., a hard-working general practitioner, or John Jones, M.I.C.E., a consulting engineer with a good training but no capital, or John Jones, works manager, or John Jones, Civil Servant, who have escaped an O.B.E. by sticking to my job, or even John Jones, a small employer making a modest income, the question may offer considerably greater difficulties, and I may be hard put to it in endeavouring to decide whether I am a " proletarian " or a " bourgeois " in the sense of a member of the capitalist class.

Indeed, my first instinct, in these circumstances, will probably be to refuse absolutely to fit myself in to any such " arbitrary " classification. If the classification will not fit me, so much the worse, I shall be inclined to say, not for me, but for the classification. And then, according to my temperament and position, I shall probably add something either about " the general public," or about the great " middle classes," or about a " third party in industry." At least, that is what " I " should almost certainly have done a few years ago, and what many of " my " class would still do to-day.

But the comfort to be extracted from such reflections and observations is, as many of the members of the social types mentioned above are finding, increasingly cold comfort. It does not help me to feel that I am a third party, if at the same time I feel that I am powerless and at the mercy of the struggle which is going on between the two principal parties in Society to-day. I share neither in the high profits of the rich, nor in the hopes and comrade-ship of Labour. I find the real value of my fixed income dwindling as profits and wages, in their struggle to maintain and increase their real share in the national product, force up prices at my expense. And I can, as a rule, see little hope of combining effectively with my peers to maintain my own position in face of the general struggle.

Moreover, I can see that this struggle is becoming more bitter, and is beginning to render impossible the continuance of the industrial system on the old basis. Especially if I am concerned directly with industry, I find the possibility of doing effective work as consultant, manager or small employer more and more interfered with by the growing hostility between capitalists and workers. If I have imagination, I am led to examine, not only my own immediate difficulties, but the basis of the economic system out of which they arise. Even if I have little imagination, I begin to cast round for some way of escape from conditions which are already unpleasant, and may soon become unbearable.

But, as soon as I do this, I am likely to find that I am compelled to make a choice. I may try for a time to act in isolation or to seek my economic ends in common only with the other members of my own calling. I may try to form a " Third Party " in industry or in politics, through some " Middle-Class Union " or " Federation of Middle-Class Workers." But experience will soon teach me, if I am capable of learning by experience, that salvation does not lie that way, and that, even if I succeed in obtaining immediate economic advantages by such action, these advantages are speedily neutralised by the rise in prices and the growing disintegration of the economic system itself, and do nothing to recall industry to efficiency of service, or to bring Society to a more reasonable way of living.

There is, therefore, an increasing pressure upon the professional, managerial and staff grades in the various industries and services, and upon the middle section of Society generally, to make a choice of allegiance, and to decide whether it will throw in its lot with the financier and capitalist sections in their struggle to maintain the existing order, or with the working-classes in their struggle to overthrow and replace it. This choice does not, of course, present itself in the same form to all the members of the grades and classes in question. It is different for the employed manager or technician, for the professonal man working on his own, for the small employer, for the small shop-keeper, for the farmer, and for many others. Nor to the consciousness of the great majority can this definite choice be said to have been as yet definitely presented at all. But, for a steadily increasing minority, the necessity of the choice is becoming obvious, and, on grounds more or less rational, the choice itself is being made.

Let us consider first the position of the technician or manager who is employed in some industry or in commerce. If he is in receipt of a really considerable salary, he still in most cases ranks himself definitely with the capitalist class, and regards himself as menaced by attacks on that class. But among the less highly paid grades of professional, managerial and administrative workers, there is a rapidly growing disposition to take up a different point of view. This tendency is greatly helped by the amazing stupidity of capitalism, which makes it underpay and tyrannise over the lower grades of its technical and administrative staffs. This question of underpayment and maltreatment gives the first stimulus to an independent point of view. The technicians and administrators begin to organise on independent lines, only to be met by a refusal by the stupid capitalists to " recognise " or negotiate with their organisa-tions. It is usually not long before an association, finding itself in this position, begins to consider the propriety of an alliance with the working-class, or before its members acting as individuals begin to vote Labour or to link up with the Labour Party or with some similar organisation.

The recent history of professional organisation in this country and elsewhere is full of examples of this kind. In France, the General Confederation of Labour has taken the initiative in forming an " Economic Council " on which the technicians and administrators are uniting with the manual workers to devise plans for a new industrial order. In America, the younger groups of " employment managers," trained in the reactionary school of " Scientific Management," are revolting towards the idea of a more democratic industrial system. In this country, organisation among professionals and " staff " workers on Trade Union lines has made vast progress. The Engineering and Shipbuilding Draughtsmen have created an almost blackleg-proof organisation, which has joined the Trades Union Congress and entered into relations with the engineering Trade Unions. The Railway Clerks' Association has passed from a purely clerical organisation into an effective association of the greater part of the " staff " grades in the railway service, including men in receipt of substantial incomes and occupying important administrative posts. The engineering, electrical, chemical, banking, shipping, insurance, law, accountancy, architectural, textile, distributive, theatrical and many other groups of staff and professional workers have formed bodies which are definitely Trade Unions and have come into more or less close relation with the general Trade Union movement. At the same time, organisation has spread with astonishing rapidity through almost every grade of the services of National and Local Government.

I do not mean to suggest that all these organisations consist of class-conscious revolutionaries, or even that they have necessarily recognised their solidarity of aim with the manual workers. I only claim that this realisation is beginning, and that the Trade Unions which they have formed are essential first steps towards the creation of an effective unity. A " brain-workers " Trade Union of this type, even if it begins by being somewhat " snobbish " in its attitude, and by seeking to emphasise its difference from an ordinary Trade Union, is likely before long to find its snobbishness slipping off from it, and its essential unity of purpose with other Trade Unions resulting in common action on a wider basis. This development has already been greatly advanced by the severe economic pressure upon the professional workers which has resulted from the increased cost of living. This economic pressure has, no doubt, been up to the present the most important cause of the advance in organisation and change in attitude among the " brain-workers."

Of course, the extent to which, and, still more, the rapidity with which, this development can take place, depends largely on the attitude of the Trade Unions of manual workers, and on the policy which they adopt. There is " snobbishness " not only among the " black-coated " and the professionals, but also among the manual workers, some of whom look askance at the attempts at organisation of persons whom they regard as belonging to the middle classes, and as playing in industry the rôle of " masters' men." This suspicion is encouraged by the attitude of some professional bodies, not of the Trade Union type, which have recently been used by the Government as recruiting agencies for blacklegs in Labour disputes such as the electricians' and railwaymen's strikes. It is still difficult for the manual workers to distinguish clearly between the Trade Unions of professional and " staff " workers and the various professional Institutes, which are in no sense Trade Unions, do not consist only of employed persons, and are still largely dominated by an anti-Labour point of view. But the distinction will have to be made, and is being made to an increasing extent, as the new type of " brain-workers' " Trade Unionism develops.

A second difficulty in the way of a full understanding by the manual worker of the brainworkers' organisations lies in the higher stage of development and self-confidence which the older Trade Unions have for the most part reached. They have got past the stage of expressing their desire to establish better relations and perfect solidarity of outlook with their employers, and have come to look forward to a time when employers, as an economic class, will no longer exist. When, therefore, they see some of the new " brain-workers' " Unions talking about better relations with capital and emphasising their purely pacific intentions, they are apt to take the view that organisations which use such language cannot be real Trade Unions, and must be allies of the employers. In taking this view they forget that, if they looked back into the history of their own organisation, they would find that in many cases, in its earlier days of struggle, when it had less power and self-confidence than now, it used exactly the same language, and showed exactly the same timidity. It is absurd to expect the new Unions to come into being as adults : they must pass through their stage of adolescence ; but, if they are handled in the right way, they will be likely to throw off the apron-strings at a very early period in their career. Indeed, a clear recognition of the function of the " brain-workers " in industry, and of the necessity of a close alliance between the workers by hand and brain, is being rapidly forced upon the manual workers' Unions by their adoption of the policy of " control." As soon as the organised workers set out, not merely to bargain collectively about wages and conditions, but to take over, as rapidly as they can, the actual productive control of industry, or, at any rate, as soon as they begin to formulate any definite plans for the assumption of control, they are at once driven to contemplate an alliance with, and the assignment of definite functions in control to, the technicians and " staff " workers connected with industry. We have seen already how this development has forced itself upon the miners in connection with their demand for national ownership and democratic control ; we have seen how it must force itself upon the railwaymen and upon other groups as soon as they are faced with a similar situation, and have to devise a definite plan for the national ownership and democratic control of the railways. The policy of control, in other words, necessarily implies the recognition, as a part of the " proletariat," of a sufficient proportion of the technical staffs of industry to be able to conduct the industries effectively in conjunction with the manual workers.

The position of the professional man working on his own is more difficult to define, both for himself and for the student of social questions. The various skilled professions in most cases include a very great diversity of economic grades. There is a wide gulf between the successful Harley Street specialist and the ordinary general practitioner, between the successful consulting engineer with large capitalist interests and the rank and file of the same profession, between the higher grades and the general run of almost all professions. Moreover, in many professions an increasing proportion of the members is becoming, either actually or virtually, employed, in the service sometimes of the local or central Government, and sometimes of big capitalist firms and combines. The doctors furnish the clearest case of this development ; for, although the full-time salaried doctors are still a small minority, the panel practitioner has to an increasing extent, whether he likes it or not, the status and problems of an employed person.

The result of this changing status of the medical profession has speedily been reflected in the attitude and policy of the various medical associations, which have become more and more like Trade Unions as the doctor has become more and more " employed." The growth of this employmental status in the professions is every day bringing their members nearer in method and policy to the " proletariat," in the enlarged sense in which the term has to be used, if it is to correspond to the real cleavage in our society at the present time.

I do not suggest that, in order that a person or group may become the ally of, or become identified with " Labour," it is essential that he or they should become employed, or should be of the family of an employed person. I only suggest that part of the momentum towards an enlarged definition of the " proletariat," under which it will be taken to include nearly all those who live by hand or brain and not by the power of wealth, comes from this tendency of the class of " employed persons " to expand. Clearly, the professional who continues to earn a reasonable living by working on his own is just as much a part of the " proletariat " in this sense as his fellow who is directly employed, and no less clearly some employed persons, who are also and primarily capitalists, do not belong to the proletariat. The drive towards Labour, politically as well as economically, as recent by-elections serve to show, is influencing the whole body of professionals, and, of course, more especially the younger elements among them, which are the most important and will determine their policy in the future. The rise in the cost of living is probably the main influence which is driving the middle-class workers towards Labour ; but it is by no means the only influence at work.

Hitherto, the new forces which are at work have had

16

least influence among the class of small employers and shop-keepers, whose members still feel for the most part that their security, such as it is, is bound up with the continuance of capitalism. But even here there are already factors making for a change of outlook. At one time, Socialist prophets used to be fond of declaring that the growing concentration of industry under capitalism would result in the elimination of the small employer, and that the big multiple shops on the one hand and the Co-operative Movement on the other, would deal a death-blow to the small shopkeeper. To-day, we can see that this has not happened, and is not likely to happen. It is true that the concentration of both industry and trade is proceeding at a constantly growing pace ; but, although this is reducing the relative importance of the " small men," it is having no considerable effect upon their absolute numbers. They survive ; but capitalist concentration is more and more subordinating them to itself, and robbing them of all real control over their occupations and over society as a whole.

We have already discussed this problem incidentally in two chapters of this book, in relation, first, to the smaller employers in the building industry, and, secondly, to the small shopkeeper. In the former case, there are already signs, in the recent Report of the " Public Service " Committee of the Building Trades Parliament, that the position is affecting the attitude of some at least of the employers in the industry. There is at present no similar organised movement among shopkeepers or on other industries ; but no one who goes up and down the country can help noticing the number of individuals of both these classes who have recently come into the Labour Party. Indeed, it may be that the preposterous Profiteering Act passed by Parliament in 1918 was not only an attempt to divert public attention from the operations of trusts and " Big Business " generally, but also had the object of setting Labour at the small shopkeeper with a view to keeping them effectively asunder.

The farmers form another group within which there are wide differences of wealth and social status. The land-owners are at present busily attempting to ensure an alliance between themselves and the farmers by appealing for Country *versus* Town. They claim, quite truly, that the past policy of Labour has paid little attention to rural problems, and they even attempt to enlist the support of the agricultural labourers against the Labour Movement on the ground that rural interests must stick together for mutual protection. There are few questions more urgent for the Labour Movement, even in this country where agriculture is relatively on a small scale, than the thinking out and formulation of an effective rural policy. The farmers do not love the landowners, and have really interests opposed to theirs ; and an effective Labour policy, based on security and control for the rural worker, security of tenure, improved farming methods, extended co-operation and fair market conditions, would speedily result in a re-grouping of the various sections. All over the world, and especially in the English-speaking countries, the farmers are becoming conscious of the power that comes of organ-isation, and in several cases a tendency on their part to ally themselves with Labour is already becoming manifest. This is plainest in Canada, where the Canadian Council of Agriculture and the various provincial Grain-Growers Organisations have become the most powerful single force in politics, and where the new Ontario Government has just come to power as the result of an alliance of the farmers with Labour. The same tendency is at work in the United States, where the Non-Partisan League has been negotiating with important sections in the Labour world. In Australia the farmers have just come to political consciousness, and the problem of their relations with Labour is beginning to be seriously considered. European Labour has not, as a rule, been happy in its attempts to formulate an agrarian policy ; but all the world over, in Russia, in America, in Italy and over the whole of Southern Europe, the problem of the relations of town workers and country workers either has forced itself, or is forcing itself, dramatically to the front. It is not everywhere the same problem ; for it appears in widely different forms in the peasant-proprietorship countries and in those where the labouring class is for the most part landless. But everywhere it has to be faced ; for even in Great Britain agriculture is important enough to wreck the chances of an effective economic democracy, unless Labour has a clear and practicable policy which it is prepared to put into effect when it comes to power. I do not pretend that I know the solution ; but clearly we must find a definition of the rural class struggle which will correspond to our amended definition of the class struggle in the towns, and a policy to fit our amended definition.

My purpose in this concluding chapter has been to draw attention to some of the factors in the class struggle proceeding in this country to-day which are obscured by the normal presentation of that struggle as purely one between the proletariat and the capitalist class. That the two protagonists are on the one side the manual workers and on the other the financiers of industry and commerce, I fully agree ; but it is fatal to ignore the many intermediate groups upon whom the issue of the struggle may easily depend. If the capitalist financiers love the acquiescence of the " brain-workers," or of a large section of them, the process of capitalist dissolution which is beginning with the increasing defection of the manual workers will be brought rapidly to a conclusion.   If the manual workers can gain the adhesion of a considerable proportion of the " brain-workers," it will become easy for them, not merely to over-throw capitalism, but to replace it, almost without friction, by a far better and more efficient social and industrial system.   To destroy without immediately replacing may at times be necessary ; but it is far better, if it can be done, to replace as we destroy.

Increasingly the real cleavage in industry and society to-day is coming to be a cleavage between the workers by hand and brain on the one side, and the *rentiers* and finan-ciers on the other.   It is the business of those who believe in social and industrial democracy to devise a policy which will enable all the elements in society which live by exer-cising a useful function to co-operate in exercising their various functions, not on behalf of a possessing or ruling class, but on behalf of the whole community.   The fore-going chapters are an attempt, in relation to certain in-dustries and services, to outline the essentials of such a policy.   They are incomplete and fragmentary, and only cover a restricted part of the field ; but they are put forward in the hope that they may help to stimulate discussion over a wider field than they actually cover.   It will perhaps be said that their greatest weakness lies in the fact that they seem to treat industry as a problem which can be isolated from the problem of social structure as a whole. I agree that it cannot be so treated in practice, and I there-fore propose to follow up this book with another in which I shall endeavour to discuss, in the same practical spirit, those problems of social organisation and policy which are concerned, not with the productive control of the various industries, but with the problems of government and administration and with the relations of the Guilds to which I look for the future productive control of industry with the general structure and working of a democratic society.

APPENDICES

APPENDIX I

MEMORANDUM ON THE CAUSES OF AND REMEDIES FOR LABOUR UNREST, PRESENTED BY THE TRADE UNION REPRESENTATIVES ON THE JOINT COMMITTEE APPOINTED AT THE NATIONAL INDUSTRIAL CONFERENCE, HELD AT THE CENTRAL HALL, LONDON, ON 27TH FEBRUARY 1919.

I. THE CAUSES OF UNREST

No one can doubt the existence in the United Kingdom at the present time of the most widespread and deep-seated unrest that has ever been known in this country. The causes of this unrest do not admit of any simple and comprehensive explanation. They are various and diverse, and different causes take the first place in different districts and among different groups of workers. The main outlines are, however, sufficiently distinct to admit of certain broad and general conclusions, and this memorandum is an attempt to describe some of the most important causes so far as they relate to economic conditions. No attempt will be made to deal with causes of a political character, although it is impossible to separate these completely from economic causes. Thus, the representation of Labour in Parliament not only has a political aspect, but also provides, under favourable conditions, the best possible safeguard for a constitutional ventilation of economic grievances, and the under-representation of Labour in the present House of Commons must therefore be classed, to this extent, among the economic factors, as well as among the political factors, in unrest. It must be remembered that throughout the war the workers have been led to expect that the conclusion of hostilities would be followed by a profound revolution in the economic structure of society. Not only social theorists, but also the most prominent spokesmen of the Government, and not a few employers, have constantly told the workers that we should never revert to the old conditions of industry, and that an altogether higher standard of life and an altogether superior status for the worker in industry would be secured as soon as the immediate burden of hostilities was removed. The Prime Minister himself has urged an official deputation from the Labour Party to be audacious, and the promises of drastic industrial change made by the Government are too numerous to chronicle. The Prime Minister's own words to the Labour Party Deputation are worth quoting. He said : —

> " I am not afraid of the audacity of these proposals. I believe the settlement after the war will succeed in proportion to its audacity. . . . Therefore, what I should be looking forward to, I am certain, if I could have presumed to have been the adviser of the working classes, would be this : I should say to them ' Audacity is the thing for you.' Think out new ways ; think out new methods ; think out even new ways of dealing with old problems. Don't always be thinking of getting back to where you were before the war ; get a really new world."

In view of the attitude now adopted by the Government in regard to industrial reconstruction, these words of the Prime Minister must be regarded as a material cause of Labour unrest.

1. LACK OF POLICY

At the present moment the workers find themselves face to face with disappointment. There is also no sign that any comprehensive policy has been prepared, or even contemplated, by the Government or by the employers, with a view to bringing about any drastic change in industry. Everywhere the workers find either the determination to revert as soon as possible to pre-war conditions in the operation of commerce and manufacture, or, where the question of reverting to pre-war conditions does not arise or concerns primarily Labour, they find that few, if any, preparations have been made for the introduction of real changes. The lack of any comprehensive industrial or economic policy on the part of the Government or the employers must therefore be regarded as one of the principal factors in the present Labour unrest.

2. THE CONTROL OF INDUSTRY

With increasing vehemence Labour is challenging the whole structure of capitalist industry as it now exists. It is no longer willing to acquiesce in a system under which industry is conducted for the benefit of the few. It demands a system of industrial control which shall be truly democratic in character. This is seen on the one hand in the demand for public ownership of vital industries and services, and public control of services not nationalised which threaten the public with the danger of monopoly or exploitation. It is also seen in the increasing demand of the workers in all industries for a real share in industrial control, a demand which the Whitley scheme, in so far as it has been adopted, has done little or nothing to satisfy. This demand is more articulate in some industries than others. It is seen clearly in the national programmes of the railwaymen and of the miners ; and it is less clearly formulated by the workers in many other industries. The workers are no longer prepared to acquiesce in a system in which their labour is bought and sold as a commodity in the Labour market. They are beginning to assert that they have a human right to an equal and democratic partnership in industry ; that they must be treated in future not as " hands " or part of the factory equipment, but as human beings with a right to use their abilities by hand and brain in the service not of the few but of the whole community.

The extent to which workers are challenging the whole system of industrial organisation is very much greater to-day than ever before, and unrest proceeds not only from more immediate and special grievances, but also, to an increasing extent, from a desire to substitute a democratic system of public ownership and production for use with an increasing element of control by the organised workers themselves for the existing capitalist organisation of industry.

3. High Prices

Among the more immediate and special causes of industrial unrest the high prices prevailing for commodities of common consumption take a prominent place. High prices in themselves cause industrial unrest, since the attempt is seldom, if ever, made to readjust wages to a higher cost of living until the workers themselves strongly press their demands. The fact that the onus of securing concessions which are necessary even to maintain Labour in its present position is always thrown upon the workers, and that strong resistance is practically always offered by the employers to such readjustments is a standing provocation to unrest, and has been a very material factor during the time of increasing prices through which we have been passing. Moreover, the workers are convinced that the high prices which have prevailed have not been unavoidable or purely due to natural causes. From the very beginning of the war period the Labour Movement has pressed upon the Government the adoption of measures designed to keep down the cost of living, and, although control over private industry has been gradually extended, it has, in most cases, not been sufficiently thorough or has been instituted far too late to check materially the rising prices, and certainly too late to prevent the amassing of huge fortunes at the public expense. The system of control which has operated during the war has meant, in the majority of cases, the fixing of prices at a level which will give what is regarded as a reasonable margin of profit to the least efficient concern, and this has meant, in case after case, the fixing of prices which leave an entirely unnecessary balance of profit to the more fortunately situated or more efficient establishments. In these circumstances unrest arises, and the workers are strongly convinced that the only way of keeping down prices is by taking production and distribution into the hands of the public itself so that the price can be fixed at such a level as to be fair in the aggregate and so that gains and losses can be distributed over the whole supply of each product. The fact, then, that control by the State has usually been instituted too late, and the further fact that, even when it has been put into operation, it has not had the effect of reducing prices because the motive of private profit has still been preserved, must be regarded as a most potent factor in aggravating unrest and confirming working-class suspicions of widespread profiteering.

4. PROFITEERING

The universal opinion among the working classes that profiteering has taken place during the war on an unprecedented scale must also be reckoned as one of the most important causes of unrest. It is, of course, impossible to produce an accurate statement of the extent and character of this profiteering, but an indication is given in the enclosures [1] of the type of fact reported in the newspapers which has been a powerful influence in convincing the public that widespread profiteering is prevalent. Indications have pointed to the fact that large fortunes have been amassed as a result of the war by many sections among the employing and financial classes. The following indications are those which have principally led to the impression that extensive profiteering has been prevalent :—

    a. The reports in the newspapers of dividends, distribution of bonus shares, distribution of dividends higher than pre-war dividends after payment of excess profits duty, and other reports showing that the prosperity of well-known firms is greater than ever before as a result of the war.

    b. The impression that large profits beyond those actually declared in the form of dividends or bonus shares have been accumulated by one or other of the following methods :—

[1] Not here reprinted

The placing of exceptionally large sums to the reserve beyond the increase in depreciation necessitated by war conditions.

The equipment, by grant or out of excess profits at the public expense, of new factories, etc., or the re-equipment of old ones, which will be in a position to earn high profits after the war.

c. The impression that the excess profits tax has operated not so as to reduce the total amount of profit obtained by the large concerns which have been in a position to secure almost what prices they chose to ask for their commodities, but to increase prices and thereby maintain profits at the same height as they would have reached if there had been no excess profits taxation.

d. The constant references in Government reports and in the newspapers, giving accounts of the progress of combination among firms which have led to the impression that " vested interests " are becoming more powerful in the community than ever, and that there is a serious danger of a great extension of private monopolies prejudicial to the public, and that the Government is steadily fostering combination among capitalists without adequate safeguards for the public interest.

e. The fact that huge combinations of capitalists have been formed during the war for the express purpose of influencing the Government, and the impression that these combinations are listened to with far more attention by Government Departments, than the representations made by Labour.

This list by no means exhausts the causes which have led the workers to believe that widespread profiteering

exists, but it would be impossible to carry the matter
further without entering into considerable detail. It need
only be said that profiteering in articles of working-class
consumption, such as food, naturally produces a more
immediate and profound impression in working-class circles
than profiteering which, although it may be even more
extensive, is not equally apparent to the ordinary man or
woman. The work of the Ministry of Food and of the
Consumers' Council has done something to diminish the
suspicion among the workers of food profiteering, but
this suspicion is rapidly reviving as a beginning is made of
the removal of food control.

5. GOVERNMENT POLICY IN RELATION TO INDUSTRY

The actions of the Government in relation to industry
since the general election have deepened the working-class
impression that profiteering is prevalent. The sale of
national ships, shipyards, and factories is strongly resented
by Labour, especially as this has taken place at a moment
when the ships might have been made of the greatest use,
in national hands, both in relieving the necessities of the
world and in preventing the creation of powerful shipping
monopolies. The shipyards might have been used to increase and develop a national mercantile marine, and the
factories, as well as the shipyards, might have been turned
to the task of useful peace-time production, and might
have been made a powerful factor for the prevention of
unemployment both during the period of dislocation and
permanently. The words used by the Minister of Labour
at the Industrial Conference on 27th February have
intensified Labour's misgivings. Sir Robert Horne
said :—

" The consideration which ultimately weighed with the Government was that the only chance of expediting matters at the present time was to restore confidence in private enterprise. . . . If the Government was regarded as a competitor in the industries which private enterprise was at present running they would never get proper work started again at all."

This is by no means the view of Labour, which holds strongly that the development of national resources under public ownership is the most urgent need of industry at the present time. The eagerness of the Government to sell the national property and its expressed determination to compete in no way with private interests in the task of production, even on such commodities as telephones, which are required by the Government itself in large numbers, and the hasty abandoning of national control over industry, without any adequate safeguards for the future protection of the consumer, have led the workers to the view that the Government's first concern is the restriction of public ownership and the restoration, at all costs, of the system of production for private profit. Moreover, the refusal of the Government to come to any decision on the question of mine and railway nationalisation, despite definite promises made during the general election, and although the solution of this question is obviously vital to the problem of industrial reconstruction as a whole, seems to show that no constructive industrial policy can be expected. Thus, disillusionment and fear of exploitation in the future on an unprecedented scale has made the workers think that their only remedy lies in taking matters into their own hands.

6. UNEMPLOYMENT

The prevention of unemployment and provision against unemployment should have been one of the first thoughts of the Government as soon as the question of industrial reorganisation began to be considered. The workers fully understood that steps were being taken to bring into immediate operation upon the conclusion of hostilities a permanent scheme both for the prevention of unemployment wherever possible and for the maintenance of the unemployed where this could not be done. They now find that no permanent provision has been made, and that the Government actually proposes to withdraw the temporary provision for the unemployed before instituting any permanent system of prevention and maintenance. The reduction of the unemployment donation before a comprehensive and permanent scheme of prevention and provision has been brought into operation, will have the effect of extending and increasing unrest. Moreover, the administration of the unemployment donation has given considerable cause for dissatisfaction, especially in the case of women, who are being compelled in case after case to take jobs in sweated industries practically at pre-war rates of wages.

We are of the opinion that the unequal distribution of wealth, which prior to the war kept the purchasing power of the majority of the wage-earners at a low level, constituted a primary cause of unemployment. During the Labour unrest debate in the House of Commons, February 1912, the Parliamentary Secretary to the Board of Trade stated that the department had particulars of wages paid to 7,300,000 work-people, and further informed the House that 60 per cent. of the wage-earners for whom they had particulars were receiving less than 30s. per week. From the Land Enquiry Committee Report, published in 1913, we learn that about 60 per cent. of the ordinary adult agricultural labourers received less than 18s. per week, a substantial percentage being in receipt of less than 15s. per week.

In 1911 the Government appointed a Royal Commission to investigate the cause of a dispute affecting railway employees. The Union representatives submitted a statement showing the rates of wages for railway war workers in 1906, as follows :—

| | | | Per cent. of total |
No. receiving £1 per week or less.			number employed.
England and Wales	.	81,300	36·7
Scotland	. .	12,960	45·2
Ireland	. .	6,650	74·5

Showing over 100,000 workers employed in an industry not affected by foreign competition not exceeding £1 per week.

Sir G. S. Barnes, Second Secretary, Board of Trade, giving evidence before a Select Committee of the House of Commons in 1913, supplied the following particulars of wages paid to women workers.

In the Sugar Confectionery trades 40·5 per cent. were receiving less than 10s. per week, with an average wage of 11s. 9d. Food preserving 44·4, with an average of 10s. 11d. The women employed in the hollow-ware trade to the number of 700 have been on strike to obtain a minimum wage of 10s. for a week of 54 hours.

In the calendering and machine ironing trade, of the women over 18 years of age working full-time 32 per cent. earned under 10s., and the average was 11s. 4d. for a 60-hours week.

17

The above particulars of wages paid covering Railway Workers, Agricultural Labourers, and a large percentage of women workers indicate that a very large body of wage-earners have received a rate of wages limiting their power of consumption to such an extent as seriously to limit the effective demand for all the essentials of life, and as a consequence unemployment has been created by under consumption.

7. Wages and Earnings

The termination of hostilities caused a sudden reduction in the earnings, though not in the wage rates, of huge classes of workers, without any corresponding decrease in the cost of living. This has, no doubt, to some extent intensified the unrest, but wage grievances are not, at the present time, responsible for more than a fraction of it. At the same time there are two aspects of the wages problem in connection with which the uncertainty of the present position is already causing serious unrest.

1. Most classes of workers have put forward demands for wage increases and the incorporation in wages of war advances, with a view not merely to maintaining their pre-war position in relation to the increased cost of living, but to improving their economic position. Failure to satisfy the universal demand of the workers for a higher standard of life will undoubtedly be followed by widespread unrest. This applies not only to the highly organised, but also to the less organised groups of workers. It is the universal opinion among the workers that every worker, no matter what the trade or occupation with which he or she is connected, is entitled

to a reasonable minimum standard of life, and that the existing slow and cumbrous methods of dealing with this problem by the gradual and piece-meal extension of the Trade Boards Act, in face of persistent obstruction and opposition, are entirely inadequate.

2. The Wages (Temporary Regulation) Act is due to expire in May. Unless steps are taken to renew it until permanent provision has been made for dealing with wage rates in the future, unrest will be gravely increased.

8. Hours of Labour

Probably the most important immediate cause of unrest is the question of hours of labour. Hours have been singularly little changed for a very long time past, and before the war demands were being made in many industries for a substantial reduction. The workers are now urgently demanding a higher standard of leisure, to be achieved by a reduction in working hours and the abolition of systematic overtime. If matters are allowed to drift, these demands will lead to serious unrest and possibly dislocation in practically every industry in the country. There is a strong opinion among the workers that the hours problem should be dealt with as a whole with a view to the formulation of some maximum limit applicable to all workers. Otherwise hours of labour will take a prominent place in encouraging unrest for a long time to come.

9. Housing

Side by side with the demand for a higher standard of life and leisure comes the demand for more and better housing accommodation. Overcrowding has been an especially serious factor in the creation of unrest in many centres during the war period, and attention was drawn to this point in the reports on Industrial Unrest prepared for the Government two years ago. . . . The rapidly growing shortage of houses at the present time, and the failure to build new houses, have done a great deal to undermine working-class confidence, and must now rank among the principal factors of unrest.

10. RECOGNITION OF TRADE UNIONS

More than one dispute recently has centred around the question of the recognition of trade unionism. Among Government employees the Police Union has been refused recognition, and serious unrest has thereby been caused. The Railway Clerks' Association only secured partial recognition from the Government by the threat of an immediate strike, and even now serious trouble is being caused by the attempts of the Railway Executive Committee and the companies to whittle down this recognition. There has been serious delay in applying the Whitley Committee's Report to any section of Government employees, and even now it has not been applied to the Civil Service, with the result that this class of workers is in a grave state of unrest. Among employees of private firms recognition is still by no means completely or fully established—a point which has been specially brought to our notice by one Association, that of the Engineering and Shipbuilding Draughtsmen, which, although it includes practically all the draughtsmen eligible for membership, is still refused recognition. Recognition is still especially defective in the workshops, and it is clear that the failure to provide for full recognition of Trade Union organisation in and out of the workshops is responsible for a good deal of unrest.

11. Lack of Representative Machinery

One reason why the existing unrest in industry lacks co-ordination and is difficult to express in concrete terms is that there exists no adequate machinery capable of giving constant expression to the co-ordinated demands of the whole of the workers. Numerous Committees and Conferences have been set up and summoned by the Government for various industrial and economic purposes. These have mostly been unsatisfactory and often of an unrepresentative character. There is an urgent demand for an elective body fully representative of Labour to advise the Government on economic and industrial policy in general. The absence of such a body is certainly one of the causes for the rapid extension of the present industrial unrest, and for its taking in some cases an indefinite and incoherent form. Until some such really representative body is brought into existence, it is to be feared that unrest will continue to possess a disorganised and largely unco-ordinated character.

12. The Attitude of the Government and the Employers

It is not possible to discuss the question of Labour unrest without drawing attention to one important factor, both as causing of unrest and as making it take unconstitutional directions. It is unfortunately the fact that it has been much more difficult to get prompt attention to industrial grievances during the war period in those cases in which the workers, from patriotic motives, have remained at work and endeavoured to act by constitutional methods than where they have come out on strike or threatened immediate and drastic action. This suicidal policy of delaying remedial action for grievances until the workers have decided to take matters into their own hands is responsible for a great deal of preventable unrest, and there is a general opinion that both employers and the Government would be wise to take steps to ensure that in future grievances, as soon as they arise, and before they reach the point of danger, should be promptly considered and dealt with on sympathetic lines.

II. REMEDIES FOR UNREST

To the foregoing statement we append certain general suggestions as to remedies. We shall follow, as far as possible, in our discussion of remedies the order of the paragraphs setting out the causes of unrest.

1. CONTROL OF INDUSTRY

(a) A substantial beginning must be made of instituting public ownership of the vital industries and services in this country. Mines and the supply of coal, railways, docks, and other means of transportation, the supply of electric power, and shipping, at least so far as ocean-going services are concerned, should be at once nationalised.

(b) Private profit should be entirely eliminated from the manufacture of armaments, and the amount of nationalisation necessary to secure this should be introduced into the engineering, shipbuilding, and kindred industries.

(*c*) There should be a great extension of municipal ownership, and ownership by other local authorities and co-operative control of those services which are concerned primarily with the supplying of local needs.

(*d*) Key industries and services should at once be publicly owned.

(*e*) This extension of public ownership over vital industries should be accompanied by the granting to the organised workers of the greatest practicable amount of control over the conditions and the management of the various industries.

2. STATE CONTROL AND PRICES

(*a*) Where an industry producing articles of common consumption or materials necessary to industries producing articles of common consumption cannot be at once publicly owned, State control over such industries should be retained.

(*b*) State control has been shown to provide some check upon profiteering and high prices, and this is a reason why it should be maintained until industries pass into the stage at which they can be conveniently nationalised.

(*c*) Many groups of capitalists at the present time are loudly claiming State assistance in re-establishing their industries upon a profit-making basis. There must be no State assistance without strict State control.

3. PROFITEERING

(*a*) A determined attempt should be made in each industry by public inquiry through Royal Commissions to elicit all the facts with regard to war profiteering.

(*b*) Organised Labour in each industry or service should

have the right of nominating half the membership of the Commission, the other half being appointed by the Government to represent interests similar to those represented by the Government nominees on the Coal Commission. The Government should also, in each case, appoint a Chairman. This principle should be adopted not only in constituting these Commissions, but also in the other Committees and Commissions proposed in this memorandum.

(c) Such an inquiry should include not only firms directly engaged in industrial production, but also subsidiary and trading concerns, and a comprehensive attempt should be made to discover the extent and effect of combination between firms, and to lay bare any tendencies towards monopolistic combination which are at present developing in British industry.

(d) In view of the enormous burden of debt which has been accumulated as a result of the war and of the methods adopted in financing the war by loan rather than by direct taxation, steps should at once be taken to remove a considerable part of this burden by a graduated levy on capital from which property up to £1000 would be exempt.

4. GOVERNMENT POLICY IN RELATION TO INDUSTRY

The policy of selling national factories, ships, and shipyards should be immediately reversed, and both the ships and the shipyards and factories should be resumed by the State and operated as national concerns in the interest of the whole community.

5. UNEMPLOYMENT, SECURITY, AND MAINTENANCE

(a) We are of the opinion that a general increase in wages by improving the purchasing power of the workers would have a general and permanent effect in the direction of limiting continuous unemployment, by bringing consumption up to something more like equilibrium with production.

(b) A special commission should be appointed immediately to investigate and report within a specified limit of time, upon the whole problem of unemployment in the widest sense, and the attention of this Commission should be especially directed to the problem of under-consumption as a cause of unemployment, and the possibility of instituting a State bonus.

(c) Pending the report of this Commission the Government should at once address itself to the task of preventing unemployment by all means within its power.

(d) We strongly urge the immediate creation of a central authority to deal with the allocation of all Government contracts in such a way as to steady the volume of employment and to co-ordinate orders given by local authorities. This central authority should co-operate closely with the National Industrial Council.

(e) A complete and comprehensive scheme of unemployment provision extending to all workers on a non-contributory basis should be instituted at the earliest possible moment, and this scheme should provide for adequate maintenance of those workers who are unemployed, and for the making up of maintenance pay to those workers who are under-employed. All unemployed workpeople under such a scheme would be entitled to a flat rate of benefit. It would, however, be desirable that there should be, in addition to the flat rate, a supplementary allowance for dependent children.

(f) This scheme should be administered directly through the trade unions, the Government maintenance pay for the unemployed being handed over in the form of a subvention to the various trade unions to administer on behalf of their own members. Where in any case direct administration through a trade union is not arranged, maintenance pay should be administered through the Employment Exchanges, but if such a system of administration is to carry any confidence the present organisation of the Employment Exchanges must be drastically remodelled, and the Exchanges must be placed under the direct control of Joint Committees equally representative of the employers and trade unions.

(g) In addition to the provision made under such non-contributory national scheme, the State should assist trade unions to provide an additional benefit out of their own funds by giving a subsidy from State funds equivalent to 50 per cent. of the amount expended by the Union on unemployment allowances.

(h) Until this permanent provision is brought fully into operation it will be essential to continue, at least on the original scale, the temporary system of unemployment donation instituted on the termination of hostilities.

(i) It is absolutely necessary to make provision for a greater degree of security on the part of the worker. The worker who is threatened with arbitrary dismissal should, in all cases, have a prior right of appeal to his fellow-workers, and wherever dismissal takes place on grounds other than those of demonstrated misconduct, the worker who is dismissed should be entitled to a payment proportionate to his period of service with the firm.

(j) Special provision should be made for the maintenance of widows with dependent children, and for the endowment of mothers, in order to prevent them from being forced into industry against the interests of society.

6. WAGES

(*a*) A higher standard of living for the whole working community is not only desirable but immediately possible.

(*b*) Every worker should be entitled by law to a reasonable minimum wage.

(*c*) Until full provisions securing this to all workers have been brought into actual and complete operation, the temporary system of regulating wages under the Wages (Temporary Regulation) Act should continue.

(*d*) The principle of equal pay for men and women should be universally applied, both on grounds of justice and in order that there may be no degrading of conditions in any occupation through the introduction of female labour.

7. HOURS OF LABOUR

(*a*) A universal reduction of hours to a maximum of eight in any one day, and forty-four in any one week, is immediately necessary, subject only to such modifications in particular industries or occupations as can be clearly proved to be necessary for the efficient carrying on of the service. All such modifications should be allowed only on condition that the terms secured to the workers in the industries so exempted from the strict operation of an Eight-Hour Act should be not less favourable on the whole than the terms accorded to workers under the Act.

(*b*) Power should at once be taken to reduce the number of hours worked below eight by a simple procedure such as that of provisional order as soon as industry has been given time to readjust itself to the new conditions.

(*c*) The eight hours which should be made a legal maximum for all workers should not prevent the workers in any trade or industry either from maintaining any better conditions which they have already secured, or from securing better conditions in the future.

(*d*) Power should be taken in any Act regulating hours where a collective agreement has been arrived at between representative organisations securing a lower maximum of hours for a particular trade or occupation, to make this lower maximum compulsory for the whole trade, including those parts of it which are unorganised or unfederated.

(*e*) Any measure regulating the hours of labour should also include provisions for the prohibition of all systematic overtime, and for the payment of all overtime worked at special rates.

(*f*) Special rates of pay should apply also to night work, Sunday, and holiday work, and night work should be abolished absolutely for women and children and, wherever possible, for all workers.

(*g*) Steps should immediately be taken for the international regulation of the hours of labour, and for the inclusion of a universal maximum in the terms of the International Charter of Labour.

(*h*) The fact that a trade has not reached a high state of organisation should not be regarded as an excuse for long hours or bad conditions of employment.

8. HOUSING

(*a*) The housing of the people must be regarded as a national responsibility, and the national resources must be utilised to the fullest extent in order to secure the immediate provision of enough houses to ensure a great general improvement in housing conditions for the whole people (*b*) If local authorities fail, under the conditions now offered by the State, to provide houses, the State must itself at once assume the responsibility of providing the houses which are necessary, or of compelling the local authorities to do so.

(*c*) Far more regard must be given than in the past both to the conditions which are necessary for the maintenance of public health and to the convenience and comfort of the working class household, and especially of the housewife.

(*d*) Provision must be made for the fullest participation of working-class representatives, including women, directly chosen by the workers, in seeing that this scheme is carried properly and completely into effect.

9. RECOGNITION OF TRADE UNIONS

All trade unions and federations and associations of trade unions recognised by the Labour Movement itself must receive full recognition both from the employers and from the State and the local authorities.

10. CREATION OF REPRESENTATIVE MACHINERY

Some national machinery fully representative of the employers and of Labour to advise the Government in relation to all issues affecting industry generally should be brought into being at the earliest possible moment. This body should possess the full confidence of Labour, and should have the most democratic constitution that can possibly be secured. Without interfering where adequate machinery already exists, such an industrial council would form a useful medium for negotiation on questions affecting mutual relations of employers and workers in general, and on all questions of general industrial and economic policy.

11. The Attitude of the Government and of the Employers

(*a*) A drastic change in the attitude of the Government Departments which deal with Labour is essential.

(*b*) It should be regarded as the duty of any Government Department employing Labour or entering into contracts which involve the employment of Labour, to ensure for all workers in its direct or indirect employment an adequate standard of life, and the best possible conditions of employment.

(*c*) Any claim or demand put forward by a body of workers should be immediately attended to, whether or not a strike has taken place and whether or not notice of strike has been given, without waiting for the organised workers to demonstrate their determination to take action. The Government should aim at being beforehand with unrest by removing all legitimate grievances as soon as they arise.

(*d*) The indefensible delay of the Ministry of Labour in setting up Trade Boards must come to an end, and the machinery of the Trade Boards Act must be put into operation at once for all the less organised trades and occupations.

(*e*) The employer, if he desires to prevent Labour unrest, should regard it as part of his responsibility to secure to all the workers whom he employs the best possible conditions of life and the earliest possible removal of all grievances.

(*f*) The habitual use now made by employers of machinery of conciliation and negotiation for the purpose of delaying the settlement of industrial demands must be discontinued.

(*g*) It is essential that all machinery of negotiation should be capable of rapid operation, and that it should in no case be used for the purpose of delaying a decision, and that with a view to ensuring that it will not be so used all awards and agreements should be made retrospective to the date of the original claim.

CONCLUSIONS

The fundamental causes of Labour unrest are to be found rather in the growing determination of Labour to challenge the whole existing structure of capitalist industry than in any of the more special and smaller grievances which come to the surface at any particular time.

These root causes are twofold—the breakdown of the existing capitalist system of industrial organisation, in the sense that the mass of the working class is now firmly convinced that production for private profit is not an equitable basis on which to build, and that a vast extension of public ownership and democratic control of industry is urgently necessary. It is no longer possible for organised Labour to be controlled by force or compulsion of any kind. It has grown too strong to remain within the bounds of the old industrial system and its unsatisfied demand for the reorganisation of industry on democratic lines is not only the most important, but also a constantly growing cause of unrest.

The second primary cause is closely linked with the first. It is that, desiring the creation of a new industrial system which shall gradually but speedily replace the old, the workers can see no indication that either the Government or the employers have realised the necessity for any fundamental change, or that they are prepared even to make a beginning of industrial reorganisation on more democratic principles. The absence of any constructive policy on the side of the Government or the employers, taken in conjunction with the fact that Labour, through the Trades Union Congress and the Labour Party, and through the various Trade Union Organisations, has put forward a comprehensive economic and industrial programme, has presented the workers with a sharp contrast from which they naturally draw their own deductions.

It is clear that unless and until the Government is prepared to realise the need for comprehensive reconstruction on a democratic basis, and to formulate a constructive policy leading towards economic democracy, there can be at most no more than a temporary diminution of industrial unrest to be followed inevitably by further waves of constantly growing magnitude.

The changes involved in this reconstruction must, of course, be gradual, but if unrest is to be prevented from assuming dangerous forms an adequate assurance must be given immediately to the workers that the whole problem is being taken courageously in hand. It is not enough merely to tinker with particular grievances or to endeavour to reconstruct the old system by slight adjustments to meet the new demands of Labour. It is essential to question the whole basis on which our industry has been conducted in the past and to endeavour to find, in substitution for the motive of private gain, some other motive which will serve better as the foundation of a democratic system. This motive can be no other than the motive of public service, which at present is seldom invoked, save when the workers threaten to stop the process of production by a strike. The motive of public service should be the dominant motive throughout the whole industrial system, and the problem in industry at the present day is that of bringing home to every person engaged in industry the feeling that he is the servant, not of any particular class or person, but of the community as a whole. This cannot be done so long as industry continues to be conducted for private profit, and the widest possible extension of public owner-ship and democratic control of industry is therefore the first necessary condition of the removal of industrial unrest.

On behalf of the Trade Union Representatives,

ARTHUR HENDERSON, *Chairman.*
G. D. H. COLE, *Secretary.*

APPENDIX II

THE MINERS' BILL—SELECT CLAUSES

THE NATIONALISATION OF MINES AND MINERALS BILL, 1919

A Bill to Nationalise the Mines and Minerals of Great Britain, and to provide for the National Winning, Distribution, and Sale of Coal and other Minerals.

Whereas it is expedient that mines and minerals should be taken into the possession of the State.

Be it enacted by the King's Most Excellent Majesty, by and with the advice and consent of the Lords Spiritual and Temporal and Commons in this present Parliament assembled, and by the authority of the same, as follows :—

1. Establishment of Mining Council

(1) For the purpose of winning, distributing, selling, and searching for coal and other minerals, there shall be established by His Majesty by Warrant under the sign manual, a Mining Council, consisting of a President and twenty members, ten of whom shall be appointed by His Majesty and ten by the Association known as the Miners' Federation of Great Britain.

(2) It shall be lawful for His Majesty, from time to time to appoint any member of the Privy Council to be President

of the Mining Council, under the name of the Minister of Mines, to hold office during His Majesty's pleasure.

(3) The Members of the Mining Council, other than the President, shall be appointed for five years, but shall be eligible for reappointment. Provided that His Majesty or the Association known as the Miners' Federation of Great Britain respectively shall have power to remove any person appointed by them and appoint some other person in his place. On a casual vacancy occurring by reason of the death, resignation, or otherwise of any of such members or otherwise, His Majesty or the Miners' Federation of Great Britain, as the case may be, shall appoint some other person to fill the vacancy, who shall continue in office until the member in whose place he was appointed should have retired, and shall then retire. The members of the Mining Council shall devote the whole of their time to the business of the Mining Council.

2. MINISTER OF MINES AND PARLIAMENTARY SECRETARY

(4) The Minister of Mines and the Parliamentary Secretary shall be responsible to Parliament for the acts of the Mining Council.

3. OFFICERS, ETC.

(4) Notwithstanding anything in any Act, order, or regulation, any society of workers, all or some of whose members are wholly or partly employed in or about mines, or in any other manner employed by the Minister of Mines, or the Mining Council, or a District Mining Council, or Pit Council, or otherwise under this Act, may be registered or constitute themselves to be a Trade Union, and may do

anything individually or in combination which the members
of a Trade Union or a Trade Union may lawfully do.
Provided further that notwithstanding any Act, order, or
regulation to the contrary, it shall be lawful for any person
employed under this Act to participate in any civil or
political action in like manner as if such person were not
employed by His Majesty, or by any authority on his
behalf.

Provided, further, that no such person shall suffer dismissal or any deprivation of any kind as a consequence of
any political or industrial action, not directly forbidden
by the terms of his employment, or as a consequence of
participation in a strike or trade dispute.

4. Constitution of Mining Council

(1) The Mining Council shall be a Corporation to be
known by the name of the Mining Council, and by that
name shall have perpetual succession, and may acquire
and hold land without licence in mortmain.

.   .   .   .

5. Transference of Mines and Minerals to Mining Council

(1) On and after the appointed day, save as in Sub-
section 3 of this Section, provided—

(a) Every colliery and mine (including all mines,
quarries, and open workings of ironstone, shale, fireclay and limestone, and every other mine regulated
under the Metalliferous Mines Regulation Acts, 1872
and 1875, but not including mines, quarries, or open
workings of minerals specified in the First Schedule to
this Act), whether in actual work, or discontinued, or
exhausted, or abandoned, and every shaft, pit, bore-

hole, level, or inclined plane, whether in course of being made or driven for commencing or opening any such colliery or mine, or otherwise, and all associated properties (including vessels, lighters, railway rolling stock, and all works, including works for the manufacture of bye-products, in the opinion of the Mining Council belonging to any mine undertaking or connected with any colliery or mine, and every house belonging to the owners of any such colliery or mine, which, in the opinion of the Mining Council, is usually occupied by workmen employed at such colliery or mine), (all of which are herein included in the expression " mine ") ; and

(*b*) all coal, anthracite, lignite, ironstone, shale, fireclay, limestone, or other mineral, excepting the minerals specified in the First Schedule to this Act, whether at present being worked or not worked, or connected or not connected with any mine, beneath the surface of the ground (all of which are herein included in the expression " minerals ") ; and

(*c*) all rights and easements arising out of or necessary to the working of any mine or the winning of any mineral, including all mineral wayleaves, whether air-leaves or water-leaves, or rights to use a shaft, or ventilation or drainage or other royalties, lordships, or rights in connection therewith, whether above or below the ground (all of which are herein included in the expression " rights ")

shall be transferred to, vested in, and held by the Mining Council in their corporate capacity in perpetuity, and shall for all purposes be deemed to be royal mines, and the minerals and rights thereof respectively.

.　　.　　.　　.　　.　　.　　.　　.

6. Purchase of Mines

The Mining Council shall purchase the mines of Great Britain in them vested by this Act (other than those which are the property of the Crown at the time of the passing of this Act, or which have been disclaimed in whole or in part in accordance with Section 5 (3) of this Act) at the price and in the manner provided by this Act.   Provided always that the value of any rights as defined by Section 5 (1) (c) of this Act shall not be taken into account in computing such price, for all of which no compensation shall be paid.

.   .   .   .

9. Ascertainment of Purchase Price

(1) The purchase price of mines exclusive of associated properties (other than mines in the possession of the Crown at the time of the passing of this Act) shall be computed subject to the provisions of Sub-sections (2) and (3) of this Section by ascertaining the average annual number of tons of minerals actually raised during the five years preceding 4th August 1914 :

Provided that as regards coal-mines in no case shall the maximum purchase price, exclusive of associated properties, be taken to be more than the following :

When 100,000 tons or less have been raised per annum on the average during such five preceding years, a capital sum equal to one year's output at 12s. per ton.

When more than 100,000 tons have been raised per annum on the average during such five preceding years, a capital sum equal to one such year's output at 10s. per ton.

(2) The Commissioners in arriving at such computation shall also have regard to the actual gross and net profits which have been made in the mine during such years or thereafter and to the amounts which may have been set aside from time to time for depreciation, renewals, or development, and to the probable duration of the life of the mine, and to the nature and condition of such mine, and to the state of repairs thereof, and to the assets and liabilities of any mine undertaking existing at the time of purchase which are transferable to the Mining Council under Section 16 of this Act.

(3) Provided further that where a coal-mine, in the opinion of the Commissioners, has not been fully developed, the amount which would be raised under full development without any increase of capital expenditure shall be taken as the average annual number of tons raised, and the maximum purchase price in such case shall be taken to be a capital sum equal to the product of such number of tons and 12s. or 10s. per ton respectively, for the purpose of ascertaining the maximum value per ton under Sub-section (1) of this Section.

10. Issue of State Mines Stock

(1) The purchase price of any mine and such of its associated properties as have been purchased, as ascertained under the provisions of this Act, shall be paid by the Mining Council in mines purchase stock to the persons who, in the opinion of the Mining Council, have established their title to such stock. Provided that an appeal shall lie to the High Court under rules to be framed by the High Court from the decision of the Mining Council as to the title of any such persons, but for no other purpose.

(2) For the purpose of paying such purchase price the Treasury shall, on the request of the Mining Council, by warrant addressed to the Bank of England, direct the creation of a new capital stock (to be called " Guaranteed State Mines Stock "), and in this Act referred to as " the stock," yielding interest at the rate on the nominal amount of capital equal to that payable at the date on which this Act received Royal Assent on what, in the opinion of the Treasury, is the nearest equivalent Government Loan Stock.

(3) Interest shall be payable by equal half yearly or quarterly dividends at such times in each year as may be fixed by the warrant first creating the stock.

.   .   .   .

11. Powers of Mining Council

(1) Subject to the provisions of this Act, it shall be lawful for the Mining Council to open and work mines and search for, dig, bore, win and deal with minerals and generally to carry on the industry of mining, distributing, vending, and exporting, together with all other industries carried on in connection therewith. Provided that it shall not be lawful for the Mining Council to lease or sell any mine or minerals or rights to any person, association, or corporation.

(2) The Mining Council may, from time to time, in such manner and on such terms as they think fit—

    (a) subject to the general consent of the Treasury, appoint or continue in employment or dismiss managers, engineers, agents, clerks, workmen, servants, and other persons ; and

    (b) construct, erect or purchase, lease, or otherwise

acquire buildings, plant, machinery, railways, tramways, hulks, ships, and other fixed or movable appliances or works of any description, and sell or otherwise dispose of the same when no longer required ; and

(c) sell, supply, and deliver fuel, coal and other products, the result of mining operations, either within or without the realm ; and

(d) enter into and enforce contracts and engagements ; and

(e) generally do anything that the owner of a mine might lawfully do in the working of the mine, or that is authorised by regulations under this Act or by this Act ; and

(f) employ local authorities for any purpose they may think necessary to carry out their duties under this Act, on such terms as may be mutually agreed.

(3) In addition to the powers conferred on the Mining Council by the last preceding sub-section, the Mining Council may, in such manner as they think fit, work any railway, tramway, hulk, ship, or other applicance for the purpose of winning, supplying, and delivering coal or other products.

.   .   .   .

12. District Mining Councils and Pit Councils

(1) The Mining Council shall, for the purpose of the carrying on and development of the mining industry, divide Great Britain into districts, and shall in each district constitute a District Mining Council of ten members, half of which shall be appointed by the Miners' Federation of Great Britain.

(2) The Mining Council may delegate to any District

Mining Council or Pit Council, such of their powers under this Act as may conveniently be exercised locally, and the District Mining Council shall upon such delegation have and exercise within their district all the powers and duties of the Mining Council as may be delegated to them.

(3) A District Mining Council shall, subject to the approval of the Mining Council, have power within their area to appoint Pit Councils for each mine or group of mines, composed of ten members, half of which shall be members of the Miners' Federation of Great Britain, and nominated by the workers of the mine or groups of mines aforesaid, and the District Mining Council may delegate to such Pit Council such of their powers concerning the immediate working or management of a particular mine or group of mines as the District Mining Council may, subject to the approval of the Mining Council, think fit.

(4) The members of District Mining Councils shall be appointed for three years, but shall be eligible for reappointment, and the members of Pit Councils shall be appointed for one year, but shall be eligible for reappointment.

13. FUEL CONSUMERS' COUNCIL AND ADVISORY CONFERENCE

(1) For the purpose of advising the Mining Council it shall be lawful for His Majesty to appoint persons, to represent the interests of consumers, to be known as the Fuel Consumers' Council.

(2) The Mining Council shall have power to convoke at such time as they think fit and under such regulations and conditions as they may prescribe, advisory conferences of representatives of District Mining Councils, and the District

Mining Councils shall have power in like manner to convoke advisory conferences of Pit Councils within their area.

(3) The expenses of the Fuel Consumers' Council, National and District Mining Conferences shall, subject to the approval of the Treasury, be paid by the Mining Council.

.   .   .   .

19. REGULATIONS

(1) The Mining Council may, from time to time, make such regulations as they think necessary for any of the following purposes :—

(a) The management of mines under this Act ;

(b) the functions, duties, and powers of the District Mining Councils, Pit Councils, and other bodies or persons acting in the management and working of mines or distribution and sale of fuel under this Act ;

(c) the form of the accounts to be kept and the balance sheets to be prepared in respect of mines under this Act ;

(d) the mode in which the sinking funds and other funds connected with mines under this Act shall be held and administered ;

(e) generally any other purpose for which, in the opinion of the Mining Council, regulations are contemplated or required.

(2) The Mining Council, before making or altering any regulations or conditions of employment, including wages, as affect workmen engaged in the mining industry, shall consult with the association known as the Miners' Federation of Great Britain, and, in the event of such representatives and the Mining Council failing to agree, the matter in dispute may be referred to arbitration on such terms as may be mutually agreed.

(3) Provided that nothing in this section shall be deemed to interfere with the right of any employed person, subject to his contractual obligations, to dispose of his labour as he wills.

20. Statutory Regulations

(1) Every mine worked under this Act shall be managed and worked subject to the provisions of the Metalliferous Mines Regulations Acts, 1872 and 1875, the Coal Mines Regulation Act, 1908, the Coal Mines Act, 1911, and any other Act regulating the hours, wages, or conditions of labour in mines.

(2) There shall be transferred to and be vested in the Mining Council all the powers and duties of the Secretary of State and of any other Government Department imposed upon them by the Metalliferous Mines Regulations Acts, 1872 and 1875, the Coal Mines Regulation Act, 1908, the Coal Mines Act, 1911, or any other Act regulating or affecting mines or the hours or conditions of labour therein.

21. Duty of Mining Council to supply Coal

(1) It shall be the duty of the Mining Council to ensure that there is a sufficient supply of fuel at reasonable prices throughout Great Britain, and for this purpose it shall be lawful for the Mining Council, or for any local authority or Government Department acting on their behalf, to establish stores and depots and to employ vehicles and to use all other necessary means for the selling of fuel and to sell fuel within the area of every local authority, and, further, for this purpose it shall be the duty of the railway companies or authorities of Great Britain

to provide such facilities for the conveyance of fuel as the Mining Council may deem necessary to enable them to carry out the duties imposed upon them by this section at rates not greater than such railway companies or authorities are now entitled to charge for the conveyance of fuel.

(2) Where the Mining Council delegates to any local authority all or any of their powers under this section, it shall be lawful for such local authority to exercise all or any of the powers of the Mining Council so delegated to them.

(3) All moneys had and received or expended by a local authority under this section shall be deemed to be had and received or expended on behalf of the Mining Council.

FIRST SCHEDULE.

Minerals excluded from this Act :—

Sandstone.	Slate.	Building Clay.
Granite.	Chalk.	Gravel and Sand
Cherts.	Flints	Igneous Rocks.

INDEX

PRINTED BY MORRISON AND GIBB LIMITED, EDINBURGH

SOCIAL THEORY

By G. D. H. COLE, M.A.

Crown 8vo, **5s.** *net*

THIS is an attempt to set out in a clear and easily intelligible form the new ideas in relation to Social Theory which are steadily gaining adherents. Special, but by no means exclusive, attention is devoted to the importance of the economic factor in Society, and to the true function of the State in relation both to the individual and to other forms of association. The book breaks new ground for the student, but is so written as to present no difficulties to the general reader.

ECONOMICS

By JAMES CUNNISON, M.A.

Crown 8vo, **5s.** *net*

THIS book is written for the general reader. It aims at a brief presentation of the underlying principles of economic life, a knowledge of which is essential to citizenship ; and it therefore avoids the technical and purely academic. While assuming in the main the peace-time conditions of Western civilization, it brings into relation with such normal conditions the war-time experience of Government control of industry.

METHUEN & CO. LTD., 36 ESSEX ST., LONDON, W.C. 2

By WILLIAM McDOUGALL, F.R.S.

AN INTRODUCTION TO SOCIAL PSYCHOLOGY

Fourteenth Edition, Enlarged. Crown 8vo, **7s. 6d.** *net*

THE social philosophy of Bentham and Mill, so long dominant in this country, was based upon the doctrine that the motive of all human action is the desire to secure pleasure or to avoid pain. That this doctrine is fallacious is now generally recognized ; but its place at the foundation of all the social sciences has not yet been filled by any consistent theory of human motives. The aim of this book is to fill the vacant place, to supply this lacking foundation-stone. In the first part the principal motive forces that underlie all the activities of individuals and of societies are defined, and the way in which they become organized in the individual mind under the pressure of the social environment is sketched in systematic outline. The second part illustrates the ways in which each of them plays its part in the life of society.

BODY AND MIND

A HISTORY AND A DEFENSE OF ANIMISM

With 13 *Diagrams. Fourth Edition. Demy 8vo,* **12s. 6d.** *net*

THIS book is designed to present a comprehensive survey of the problem of the relations between body and mind. It is shown that, in spite of the efforts of many philosophers to provide alternative solutions, we are still confronted with the dilemma, materialism or animism ; it is shown also that the issue between the rival doctrines cannot be decided by metaphysical reasoning, but only by appeal to empirically established facts.

METHUEN & CO. LTD., 36 ESSEX ST., LONDON, W.C. 2